# HOW TO
# CRACK THE MORTGAGE CODE

**DISCOVER THE 19 GREATEST SECRETS TO PAY OFF YOUR MORTGAGE FAST AND SAVE HUNDREDS OF THOUSANDS OF DOLLARS NOW**

BY

**E. WRIGHT DAVIS, JD**

**"The Foreclosure Doctor"**

# Copyright

# Waiver of Legal Liability

# About the Author
# E. Wright Davis

A member of the State Bar of Georgia for 40 years, a trial lawyer, mortgage broker, real estate investor, realtor and title insurance company president.

The author and creator of five real estate investment courses and has developed an online real estate law course for a major university.

As a state supreme court certified mediator in two states, he understands real estate dispute resolution and foreclosure resolution.

Is the author of four books; *Legal Vengeance* (fiction), *Mega Mortgages, How to Crack the Mortgage Code* and *Getting Started in Creative Real Estate Investing.*

For ten years he was a state licensed real estate salesperson and mortgage broker instructor.

Served as a U.S. Delegate to the U.S.–China Conference on Trade Investment and Economic Law in Beijing China, and was selected as One of Five Outstanding Men of Georgia by the Georgia Jaycees.

**http://how-to-pay-off-mortgage-early.com**

# Acknowledgements

I wish to express my deepest gratitude to the following people who helped make this book possible:

To Gail White of Tailored PC Documents, to whom I am greatly appreciative for her word processing, organizational and publishing skills. (www.tailoredpcdocuments.biz)

And to my wife, Cynthia, whose talent and computer skills made this book come together.

And to my students who have taken my investing courses, Mega Mortgages, Cracking the Mortgage Code, Calculator Power, Getting Started in Creative Real Estate Investing, and my students in the real estate salesman and mortgage broker licensing courses throughout the years who gave me the inspiration and ideas for this book.

**http://how-to-pay-off-mortgage-early.com**

# How To Crack The Mortgage Code

## Table of contents

| Topic | Page |
|---|---|

## How to Crack the Mortgage Code

## The 8 Mortgage Myths

# Table of contents...continued

# Table of contents...continued

# For The Investor

# Table of contents...continued

# Introduction

Millions of people are losing their homes through foreclosure. There is a mortgage crisis in this country that we haven't seen since the Great Depression of the 1930's. As this book is written, 11.8 million bankcards are delinquent, and foreclosure filings topped 3 million last year.

There are many reasons; the blame agents are busy pointing their fingers at all the possible causes, and who may be responsible. There are those who blame the loose lending standards of the banks and mortgage companies making the loans. Others fault the adjustable rate mortgage. Others blame the current economic conditions, and are begging for a bailout by the taxpayers. The purpose of this book is not to affix the blame, but to provide a solution or solutions. There are hundreds of books, seminars, and courses on how to obtain a mortgage, and what you need to know to qualify for real estate financing.

To this author's knowledge, there is no comprehensive manual, book, or course, which teaches you how to pay your mortgage off fast once it is created. There have been many different methods taught through the years on how to pay a mortgage off faster, utilizing one method or another. No such book exists which brings all the methods together in one book. This book attempts to accomplish that objective.

There are those clamoring for a government bail out of the mortgage industry, and for legislation to bail out the homeowner in foreclosure. Prosecutors are aggressively prosecuting fraudulent mortgage activities. These solutions are like band-aids on cancer. They will not work in the long run.

The solution is simple, but not easy. The banking and mortgage industry cannot, and will not, provide the solution because they are financially benefiting from the problem.

**The answer is simple: PAY THE MORTGAGE OFF! I REPEAT: PAY THE MORTGAGE OFF!**

Everyone is taught to believe, either rightfully or wrongly, that the only way to pay off a mortgage is to make monthly payments for 30, 25, 20, or 15 years- the traditional way. This book will dispel that myth, and show homeowners how to pay off their home mortgages in half the time, or sometimes in as little as 5 years on a 30-year mortgage, while saving hundreds of thousands of dollars in interest payments. Some of these methods will even show you how to get someone else to pay your mortgage payments for you.

Read this book with an open mind from this page until the end. Work through the examples, study the charts, and experiment with the software found online at:

**http://how-to-pay-off-mortgage-early.com**

I can assure you that there is no greater feeling than sleeping in a home at night that you own. Again, the solution is to "**PAY THE MORTGAGE OFF**".

# How to Crack the Mortgage Code

# The 19 Greatest Secrets to Pay
# Off Your Mortgage Fast

Most homeowners and real estate investors are truly amazed at how easy it is to pay off a real estate mortgage within 5 to 7 years rather than the usual 15, 20, or 30 years. Most people do not understand how the principle of time-value of money works. They do not realize how simple it really is, and many simply will not take the time to learn it. Don't let that be you.

There are those in the investment field who advise not to pay off a mortgage because of investment considerations and tax reasons. They contend that if you can get a higher yield by investing those extra dollars in other investments than you can get by paying your mortgage off early, then you should not pay off your mortgage. These "investment counselors" further proclaim that the interest deduction is the largest tax write-off for most people, and to eliminate it will result in the tax payer paying much higher income taxes. This author contends that both propositions are erroneous.

The techniques contained in this book will show how easy it is to pay off a mortgage without utilizing the expensive mortgage programs sold by some banks and mortgage companies. It is a myth that your mortgage is your largest tax deduction because people with less than $10,900 in yearly mortgage interest payments write off nothing at all. The tax deduction is likewise false because the maximum you could save with the tax write off on your mortgage interest is 35% of the interest. It absolutely amazes me that some individuals in the real estate and banking professions advise people to spend a dollar to get a tax write off of thirty five cents. I don't want that to happen to you.

This reminds me of the story of the two country boys who were in the business of selling watermelons. They were selling their watermelons for fifty cents each. Business was a little slow so they came up with the brilliant idea to sell them two for a dollar. This way they could double their volume. This is the same logic of those who advocate a big mortgage so you can get the tax write-off.

I am a strong proponent of real estate investment when it is done correctly. There are two ways I am aware of to increase the value of real estate. The first one is to increase the value through appreciation. This is done either by inflation, making improvements to the real estate, or by changing the use, thereby potentially increasing the cash flow. The second method is to reduce and/or eliminate any indebtedness against the real estate. In these times of low appreciation and rapid devaluation, you will want to invest in debt reduction, the second method.

This book is intended to show the reader the various techniques to reduce the debt against real estate at an accelerated pace. Some of the methods discussed here are well known, and are fairly simple to implement. Others may not be as familiar to you and will require some study. All the techniques work. Some of these techniques can be used in conjunction with others. Some will require some understanding of the principles of compound interest and the time value of money, together with a little knowledge of the financial calculator. The calculations in this book were calculated on the Texas Instruments Business Analysis II Financial Calculator. However, the reader will not require a financial calculator in order to implement and utilize these techniques.

# THE TEXAS INSTRUMENTS BA II PLUS
# FINANCIAL CALCULATOR

# Notes:

# The Time Value of Money

## The secret behind the techniques.

*"Compound interest is the 8<sup>th</sup> wonder of the world"*- Albert Einstein

Money has value over time. The two concepts- money and time- are interrelated and one cannot function without the other. The purchasing power of a dollar today is worth more than the purchasing power of the dollar received in the future. Money loses buying power over time because of inflation. This is because you can invest a dollar today and earn a return or what is called a yield. Which means money is worth more ten years ago because of inflation. Past dollars invested have more buying power than dollars invested today. For example, if you invested a dollar ($1.00) today and earned ten (10%) percent interest, you would have $1.10 at the end of the year.

A lender charges for loss of buying power over time by charging what is called interest. Interest is calculated as a percentage of the remaining unpaid principal balance of the loan over a defined period of time. The dollar amount of interest is a function of three variables: (1) the interest rate (2) the amount borrowed (principal) and (3) the time period of the loan.

There are two types of interest that can be charged: "simple" and "compound."

Simple interest is calculated as follows: principal x interest rate x time. For example, if you borrowed $1,000 for 12 months at 10% simple interest, your interest would be:

Interest= $1,000 x 10% x 12 months = $100 for the 12 months.

Compound interest is the interest that accrues on both the principal and the past-unpaid accrued interest. When interest is compounded, interest is earned for each period on the principal and on the accumulated interest for the preceding periods.

For example, if you borrowed $1,000 for 12 months at 10% compound interest, your total payments would be $87.92 per month x 12 months = $1,054.99.

Financial calculators use a mathematical formula to discount today's dollars to the equivalent future dollars. This time value of money calculation determines the loss of future buying power of money paid in the future.

To determine this number, we use five financial keys on the calculator:

| N | I/Y | PV | PMT | FV |
|---|-----|----|-----|----|

They represent the following elements of a time-value of money calculation.

**N** = the number of payments remaining

**I/Y** = effective interest rate per compounding period

**PV** = present value of today's dollars

**PMT** = the periodic payment amount

**FV** = future value of the dollars

What are the key time-value of money characteristics? There are four basic characteristics that create a higher value today: (1) higher interest rate, (2) higher present value amount, (3) shorter length of time to maturity, and (4) more frequent compounding periods.

There are four basic characteristics that create a lower value today: (1) lower interest rate, (2) lower present value amount, (3) shorter length of time to maturity, and (4) less frequent compounding periods.

Our parents always taught us to save our money for the future, or "the rainy day" as they called it. Nobody listened. But, what is the value, or should I say, the cost of not following parental advice?

Let's take an example. Suppose you started investing $100 per month at age eighteen at an 8% return every month until you reached age 30, and then you stopped investing. You simply left the money alone, accumulating interest at 8% until you retired at age 65. What would be the difference if you started investing $100 per month at age 30, and continued to invest $100 per month, every month, at 8% until you retired at age 65? If you started at age 18 and quit at age 30, the total sum would be $1,020,136.80. If you started at age 30 and quit at age 65, the sum would be $229,388.25, a whopping difference of $790,748.55.

| N | I/Y | PV | PMT | FV |
|---|---|---|---|---|
| Start at Age 18 and Stop at Age 30 | | | | |
| 144 | 8 | 0 | 100 | 24,050.84 |
| (12 Years) | | | | |
| | | | | |
| N | I/Y | PV | PMT | FV |
| 564 | 0 | -24,050.84 | 0 | 1,020,136.80 |
| (47 years from age 18 to 65) | | | | |
| | | | | |
| Start at Age 30 and Stop at Age 65 | | | | |
| N | I/Y | PV | PMT | FV |
| 420 | 8 | 0 | 100 | 229,388.25 |
| (35 years) | | | | |

# Notes:

# The Power of Compounding

I always like to begin my seminars by asking the question, "Which would you rather have, a million dollars ($1,000,000) today or a penny doubled every day for 30 days?" Some people immediately opt for the million dollars ($1,000,000) now, having a little knowledge of the time value of money. Others opt for a penny doubled every day for 30 days. I ask you, "What would you prefer?" Maybe this illustration will provide the answer for you.

### DOUBLE A PENNY EVERY DAY FOR 30 DAYS

| | | | |
|---|---|---|---|
| Day 1 | $.02 | Day 16 | $655.36 |
| Day 2 | $.04 | Day 17 | $1,310.72 |
| Day 3 | $.08 | Day 18 | $2,621.44 |
| Day 4 | $.16 | Day 19 | $5,242.88 |
| Day 5 | $.32 | Day 20 | $10,485.76 |
| Day 6 | $.64 | Day 21 | $20,971.52 |
| Day 7 | $1.28 | Day 22 | $41,943.04 |
| Day 8 | $2.56 | Day 23 | $83,886.08 |
| Day 9 | $5.12 | Day 24 | $167,772.16 |
| Day 10 | $10.24 | Day 25 | $335,544.32 |
| Day 11 | $20.48 | Day 26 | $671,088.64 |
| Day 12 | $40.96 | Day 27 | $1,342,177.28 |
| Day 13 | $81.92 | Day 28 | $2,684,354.56 |
| Day 14 | $163.84 | Day 29 | $5,368,709.12 |
| Day 15 | $327.68 | Day 30 | $10,737,418.24 |

If you took the $1 million today, you would be short-changing yourself by $9.7 million.

# Notes:

# THE 8 MORTGAGE MYTHS

# Myth #1

## The only way to pay off our mortgage is according to the amortization schedule.

Why have we been led to believe that our mortgage payments must fit a schedule of 15, 20, or 30 years? The answer is obvious. The banks have designed it that way for maximum profits to them. What is the cost of a $100,000 mortgage at 6% interest payable over 30 years as opposed to 20 years or 15 years?

(Let's go to the financial calculator a minute.) A $100,000 mortgage at 6% interest for 30 years or 360 months has a monthly payment of principal and interest of $599.55. If one would pay this over the life of the mortgage, the payments would total $215,838.19. A 20-year mortgage of the same principal amount and interest rate would cost $171,943.45, and a 15-year mortgage of the same principal and interest rate would cost $151,894.23.

What is the penalty if you pay off your mortgage early? There is none unless your note has a pre-payment penalty. These generally limit prepayments of up to 20% of the principal in any one year without a penalty and the penalties go away after 2 to 3 years. The current tax code allows a deduction as interest for any prepayment penalties paid. Congress allows an income tax deduction for interest paid on your home mortgage up to certain limits.

Look at your amortization schedule, and determine how long it will take you to pay off just $2,500 of the principal of your $100,000 mortgage at 6% interest amortized over 30 years. It takes 24 months. The cost to amortize $2,500 is $14,221.34. Let's look at the ridiculous (or maybe not so ridiculous) example of paying off the same $2,500 principal with a credit card with an interest rate of 21% (not uncommon in today's market). The monthly payments would be $128.46 per month, and the total cost would be $3,083.14. The cost difference is $11,138.20, and 12 months. Suppose you applied that $11,138.20 to the principal of your mortgage. You would be saving approximately 89 payments and $53,413.96.

House Loan: $100,000
Interest Rate: 6.0%
Term: 30 years
Payment: $599.55
Loan balance after 24 months: $97,468.25
Interest Paid: $11,857.44
Principal Paid: $2,531.75
Total payments paid: $14,389.20

If you are paying on a mortgage, the time value of money is your ENEMY. If you are receiving mortgage payments, the time value of money is your FRIEND .How much of your mortgage is going toward interest, and how much toward principal? Look at the chart on the next page and you will see that almost all of your payments are going toward interest payments during the first half of the mortgage. Do you suppose it was designed that way?

**Fact to remember:**

**If you pay off your mortgage according to the amortization schedule provided by your lender, it will cost you hundreds of thousands of dollars in interest.**

# Loan Balance

| 30 Yr Mortgage | 5 years | 10 years | 15 years | 20 years | 25 years | 30 years |
|---|---|---|---|---|---|---|
| **Interest Rates** | | | | | | |
| 6% | 93% | 84% | 71% | 54% | 31% | 0% |
| 7% | 94% | 86% | 74% | 57% | 33% | 0% |
| 8% | 95% | 88% | 77% | 60% | 36% | 0% |
| 9% | 96% | 89% | 79% | 63% | 39% | 0% |
| 10% | 97% | 91% | 82% | 66% | 41% | 0% |

| 25 Yr Mortgage | 5 years | 10 years | 15 years | 20 years | 25 years | |
|---|---|---|---|---|---|---|
| **Interest Rates** | | | | | | |
| 6% | 90% | 76% | 58% | 33% | 0% | |
| 7% | 91% | 79% | 61% | 36% | 0% | |
| 8% | 92% | 81% | 64% | 38% | 0% | |
| 9% | 93% | 83% | 66% | 40% | 0% | |
| 10% | 94% | 85% | 69% | 43% | 0% | |

| 20 Yr Mortgage | 5 years | 10 years | 15 years | 20 years | | |
|---|---|---|---|---|---|---|
| **Interest Rates** | | | | | | |
| 6% | 85% | 65% | 37% | 0% | | |
| 7% | 86% | 67% | 39% | 0% | | |
| 8% | 87% | 79% | 41% | 0% | | |
| 9% | 89% | 71% | 43% | 0% | | |
| 10% | 90% | 73% | 45% | 0% | | |

# Notes:

# Myth #2

## Late payments: it's okay to pay your mortgage payment on the 14th of the month because the late penalty "begins" on the 15th.

This is a false assumption because the interest is still running on the loan from the first of the month and is added back to the principal. Wouldn't it be wonderful if interest stopped running when the bank closed its doors every afternoon? Have you ever wondered why there are so many bank holidays? As long as they have your money, they are making interest on it.

Amortization schedules are only accurate if the payment is made on the same day each month. If the payment is one day late, more of the payment will go to interest, and less to principal. The effect of continued late payments, aside from the late fees, is that the payer is going to pay off the note over a longer period of time than the amortization schedule will show.

The payer's daily interest for the current month is the "balance due" times the annual interest. You divide this figure by 365. This is the daily interest. Multiply the daily interest by the number of days the payer is late that month. This is added back to principal.

Using our example of a $100,000 loan at 6% interest rate amortized over 30 years, our monthly payment would be $599.55 per month. So if we multiply $100,000 by 6% we get $6,000. This is our annual interest. We divide this by 365 to get our daily interest of $16.44 per day. We multiply our daily interest of $16.44 times the 14 days we are late and get $230.14. This is added back to our principal. Assuming a $100,000 loan balance, this will add $230.14 back to our principal. This will give us a new loan balance of $100,230.14, and extend the amortization of the debt to 362.33 months. This will cost the mortgage payer an additional $1,396.95. Do bankers hate it when you pay your mortgage on the 14th of the month? We think not. Pay it on the 15th however, and they collect the additional late payment penalty plus the interest, which is added back to the principal.

**Facts to remember:**

1. Amortization schedules are only accurate if your payment is made on the exact day it is due every month.

2. Making your payment even one day late will cost you thousands of dollars

# Notes:

# Myth #3

## The "Interest is Tax Deductible".

This is the argument put forth by those who do not understand the tax code. Does it make sense to spend a dollar to deduct a maximum of thirty-five cents? If you increase the amount of your mortgage, you will be able to deduct more interest at thirty-five cents (in most cases, only fifteen cents) per dollar of interest paid. I wonder what would happen to the mortgage industry if Congress rewarded those for getting out of debt by allowing a deduction for each dollar of principal that is paid ?

This myth is further perpetuated by those who proclaim that your mortgage interest is your largest tax deduction, when the truth is that people with less than $10,900 in annual mortgage interest write off nothing at all, and others write off very little.

This myth is even further perpetuated by those who tell us not to pay off our mortgages if we can invest our mortgage payments at a higher yield. Let's look at an example. You have a $100,000 mortgage, payable at 6% interest over 30 years (360 months), and a monthly payment of $599.55. If we invested the $599.55 per month x 12 months or $7,194.60 per year at 8% yield, our profit would be $575.57 for the first year. Assume you were in the 25% tax bracket. Your taxes, without deducting any state income taxes, would reduce your profit to $431.68 per year. If we invested the same $7,194.60 and paid it against the principal balance of the above mortgage, we would save (eliminate) 61.85 mortgage payments or $599.55 x 61.85 months or $37,082.20. Invest the same $7,194.60 at 18% and you get $1,295.03. Deduct 25% of that for taxes, and your net is $971.27. Can an investment even at an 18% yield save you 61.85 mortgage payments? What is the better investment of your dollars?

## How Much Of A Deduction Are You Really Getting From Your Home Mortgage Interest Deduction?

Those who promote the idea that you need to go into debt by getting a mortgage on your home because the interest is deductible haven't read the Internal Revenue Code lately. Let's look at the facts surrounding this myth. Let's take the typical family of four with a first year home mortgage of $185,000 with 360 payments at 6% interest, and payments of $1,109.17 per month. The couple had paid $13,310.04 in mortgage payments. The amount of that which is "deductible" interest is $11,026.84. Let's look at the tax consequences.

|  | With Interest Deduction | Without Interest Deduction |
|---|---|---|
| Adjusted Gross Income | $61,600.00 | $61,600.00 |
| Itemized Deduction | $11,026.84 (Mortgage interest) | $10,700.00 (2010 Standard Deduction) |
| Personal Exemption (Family of four: $3,400 x 4) Line 42, Form 1040 | $13,600.00 | $13,600.00 |
| Taxable Income Line 43, Form 1040 | $36,973.00 | $37,100.00 |
| Tax (Using IRS Rate Schedule) | $ 4,763.00 | $ 4,782.00 |
| **Difference** | | **$ 19.00** |

Our typical family of four has spent $13,310.04 in mortgage payments in order to save $19.00 in taxes. What would be the result if they had invested the same amount of money they spent on mortgage interest in a mutual fund, and not have had to put their home at risk?

Just over two-thirds of all taxpayers, including most renters, do not itemize their deductions because they do not earn enough. They simply take the "standard deduction." The mortgage deduction does not help them.

**Facts to remember:**
1. **You must have $10,900 in interest before you can deduct anything.**
2. **Two-thirds of taxpayers don't deduct interest.**

# Myth #4

## The Greatest Fraud!: Interest is paid in arrears.

If you have ever been a tenant, did you pay your rent on the first of the month or on the last day of the month? You paid on the first day of the month, hopefully. Rent is always paid in advance, unless you happen to be a landlord with tenants who pay late.

Is this true with mortgage payments? Have you ever been to a real estate closing where the closing agent hands you a piece of paper or a coupon book and tells you to make your first mortgage payment in 30 to 45 days? Why is that, you wonder? Maybe, they see that you have so many dollars in closing costs that they are just trying to give you a break. Don't count on it. The lender is trying to make as much interest from you as possible. And how much interest is that? You might be surprised.

When you make your first mortgage payment, you are already in arrears on your mortgage. It was designed that way. Thus, the term, "interest paid in arrears." If you paid your first mortgage payment on the day you signed the mortgage note, how much would you owe in interest? Nothing! All your payment would be applied to principal. Why is this so important? Look at the impact of paying your first payment on the day of closing. If we have a $100,000 mortgage, payable at 6% interest over 360 months (30 years), our monthly payment would be $599.55.

If you paid the first payment of $599.55 on the day of closing, all of the payment would be applied to principal and none towards interest. Thus, your loan balance at the closing would be $99,400.45. What is so significant about this? It is significant because you would have saved 5.95 monthly payments or $3,567.33. The higher the principal amount borrowed, and the higher the interest rate, the higher the savings. As you can see, the first month can be very expensive. If you paid your mortgage payment as you paid your rent when you were a tenant, you would be ahead of the game.

House Loan: $100,000
Interest Rate: 6.0%
Term: 30 Years
Payment: $599.55 month
Total Principal Paid: $100,000
Total Interest Paid: $112,868.42

If first payment is paid at closing:
Number of payments remaining:  354.05
Total monies saved: $3,567.33

**Fact to remember:**

**Paying your first mortgage payment 30 to 45 days after closing as suggested by the lender will cost you thousands of dollars**

# Notes:

_____

_____

_____

_____

_____

_____

_____

_____

# Myth #5

## Inflation vs. Debt reduction:
## "The Greater Fool Theory"

This is the greatest myth of the 21st century. Many investors and homebuyers have been caught in this trap. Buy at whatever price the seller demands. Inflation will drive up the value, and another fool will come along and buy it from you at a higher price. What has happened in the last few years is a prime example of the greater fool theory. Investors and homebuyers have seen their homes and investments fall in value, and many into foreclosure because the values of real estate have dropped. The property value goes down in value, and the equity has been eliminated. I am by no means against purchasing real estate for investment. However, we seemed to have forgotten the other half of the equation, the mortgage debt.

You have little control over inflation. You can force inflation on real estate by improving the property, i.e. rehabbing, or by rezoning, or changing the use. However, generally you have no control over real estate value.

You do have control over the key element that many have completely ignored until the foreclosure crisis raised its ugly head. You can control the payment of the mortgage debt. If real estate drops in value like in recent times, what is the danger if there is no debt on the property? The inflation cycle will return, and real estate will go up in value again. What happens when real estate goes up in value and there is little or no debt against the property? The property is more valuable, and the owner can be more flexible in the method by which it is sold.

**Facts to remember:**
1. **You have very little control over the inflationary value of your home.**
2. **You do have control over the debt owed on your home.**

# Notes:

# Myth #6

## Prepayment Penalty

The prepayment penalty is a scare tactic used by many lenders to encourage the home-owner not to pay off his mortgage, thus continuing to let the bank reap insane profits. Let's analyze the prepayment penalty issue.

A typical prepayment penalty clause provides, *"In the first two years if you make a pre-payment, which exceeds 20% of the original principal amount of the loan in any 12-month period, you must pay a prepayment charge equal to 6 months advance interest on the amount prepaid, which is in excess of 20% of the principal amount of the loan within the 12-month period. After 2 years, there is no prepayment penalty."*

For example, if your original mortgage was $150,000, you could pay $30,000 per year with no penalty. If you paid, for example, $35,000 principal in any of the first two years, the penalty would be 6 months interest on the $5,000 difference, or $300.

How long does it take to pay $30,000 principal on a $150,000 mortgage at 6% interest over 360 months (30 years)? The payments would be $899.33 per month. It takes an unbeliev-able 139.43 months to pay a principal balance of $30,000 on the above loan. What is the cost? It takes 139.43 months times the monthly payment of $899.33, or $125,393.58. Does the prepayment penalty scare you anymore? It probably makes you angry that a lender would even put such a nuisance clause in a mortgage note. If your lender insists upon a prepayment penalty, show him the arithmetic, and move on to the next lender. Besides, the interest penalty is de-ductible, isn't it? This is another farce, which you already know about by now. V.A. and FHA loans do not have prepayment penalties.

House Loan: $150,000
Interest Rate: 6.0%
Term: 30 years
Payment: $899.33 month

Loan balance after 139.43 payments: $120,000.00
Total Paid: $125,392.99

**Fact to remember:**

**The prepayment penalty is a fraud on the mortgage payer.  It costs more money <u>not</u> to prepay your mortgage.**

# Notes:

_____

_____

_____

_____

_____

_____

_____

_____

_____

# Myth #7

## I must use a bank, mortgage company, or commercial lending institution to finance my home.

Most homeowners have been led to believe that the traditional lending institutions such as banks, mortgage companies, and commercial lending institutions are the only sources of real estate financing. Very little is known of the tremendous opportunities which exist within the owner-financing arena.

Sellers simply will not entertain the idea of owner financing for several reasons. First, and primarily, is that they need a large sum of cash immediately to invest in another property, or especially to pay off other indebtedness. They do not want to receive monthly payments, and often fear the possibility of having to take back the property they sold in a foreclosure proceeding.

Property sellers are unaware of the market for seller financed notes and mortgages. These instruments are often referred to in the investing industry as "owner carry-back" financing or "paper."

There is a whole industry of purchasers of this real estate "paper", both institutional and private. Just like the secondary market in traditional financing, such as Fannie Mae, Ginny Mae, and Freddie Mac, there are both private and institutional investors in seller financed "paper."

These privately created real estate notes can be sold, either in whole or in part, either at the time of closing in a simultaneous transaction, or at a later date after closing. This works just like conventionally financed real estate notes that are sold at a discount to Fannie Mae, Ginnie Mae, and Freddie Mae.

For example, Sam and Sue Seller had their house on the market for over 18 months. They had a few nibbles, but the only viable purchasers could not qualify for conventional financing. They were firm on their selling price of $277,800.00. They then decided to run an advertisement in their local newspaper, asking full price, but agreeing to owner finance. They quickly found a buyer who was willing to put 10% down if Sam and Sue would finance the balance of $250,000 at 6% interest, for 360 months, with payments of $1,498.88 per month.

Prior to closing, Sam and Sue located a buyer of real estate notes who offered to purchase the first 60 payments of their $250,000 note for $62,500. That is, they would sell one-fourth of the payments (60 payments) for one-fourth of the principal balance, leaving Sam and Sue a balance on the note of $187,500. The note buyer also agreed to purchase all or part of the remaining payments at a later date if Sam and Sue needed some more money.

At closing, Sam and Sue would receive $27,800 of the $75,000 they needed as a down payment (10%) for another house, plus $62,500 for the first 60 payments of their note, for a total of $90,300. They would also have a remaining balance on their note of $187,500, for a total sale price of $277,800, their original asking price. You might say, "But they had to take a discount because they did not get all of their money up front". True, but if they elected not to sell the remaining payments, they would start collecting $1,498.88 each month in 61 months for a total of 270 months and $404,696.60. If the buyers decided to refinance or sell the house, they would be paid the remaining balance in full, provided Sam and Sue included a non-assumption clause in the note and mortgage.

Owner Financed Mortgage:
House Loan: $250,000
Interest Rate: 6.0%
Term: 30 years
Payment: $1,498.88

Loan balance after 60 payments: $232,635.89
Amount of principal paid after 60 months: $17,364.11
**Facts to remember:**

**1.  Owner financing is an overlooked alternative to real estate financing.**

2. **There is an industry which purchases owner financed mortgages which is an alternative to government backed conventional financing such as FHA, VA, Fannie Mae, Ginnie Mae and Freddie Mac.**

# Notes:

_____

_____

_____

_____

_____

_____

_____

_____

_____

_____

# Notes:

# Myth #8

## Invest your money at a higher yield rather than paying off your mortgage.

When we were kids, we built rabbit trap boxes, and always put a carrot in the box as bait. The rabbit, looking for an easier, softer way to get fed, always went for the carrot rather than forage in the fields for the more difficult to find wild food. This same principle applies to investing.

Many financial planners have advised their clients to borrow as much as they can from the equity of their homes, and invest the proceeds in investments, "which yield" a higher return than the interest rate they are paying on their mortgage".

For example, if one were to borrow the equity out of his home at a 6% interest rate, and invest in an S and P 500 fund, which has consistently yielded 9% over the years, he would profit on the difference by 3%. The assumption is that one will net the spread of 3%. While the S and P has shown a predictable return over the years, it, like all investments, has had its good years, and its bad years (2008). The real problem, however, is that these financial advisors sometimes fail to advise their clients of the tax consequences and risks of such investments.

Let's look at an example. Suppose you were able to borrow $50,000 from the equity of your home using a home equity line of credit (HELOC). If the interest rate on the HELOC were 6%, interest only, computed annually, the interest due would be $3,000 per year. If you invested the $50,000 in an S and P 500 fund at 9%, you would receive $4,500 for a net profit after paying the interest on the HELOC of $1,500.

The financial advisors often fail to warn their clients that the $1,500 is taxable. If you are in a 30% tax bracket, you will pay $450 in taxes at ordinary income tax rates, or $225 at capital gains rates. You would net only $1,050 to $1,275 of the profit. You would also incur the risk of losing your home in a foreclosure if a disaster struck, and you were unable to make the payments.

What would this loan really cost you? If you borrowed $50,000 at 6% for 5 years, your payments would be $3,000 per year in interest, assuming the rate did not increase. Also, a big caveat, (big legal word for DANGER), one has to qualify for the HELOC each year. If you were late one month for whatever reason, and the bank decided to call it due, you might not be able to pay the balance, thus possibly jeopardizing losing your home.

What would be the cost if you utilized a regular fully amortized mortgage? A $50,000 mortgage at 6% interest over 360 months (30 years) would cost you $299.78 per month. A 20-year mortgage would cost $358.33 per month, and a 15-year mortgage would cost $421.93 per month.

Yes, the interest would be deductible, but as we have already seen, you would be paying $1.00 to get a $.15, $.28, or $.33 deduction- hardly smart economics.

**Facts to remember:**
1.  **Investing your funds in alternative investments or using the equity in your home to invest can be not only costly but risky.**
2.  **Income earned from alternative investments is taxable while money saved by paying off your mortgage is not.**

# Techniques

# Technique #1

## This simple technique will save you at least 6 months of mortgage payments and won't cost you a cent.

How many real estate closings have you attended where you were handed a mortgage payment coupon by the closing agent and you were told that your first mortgage payment was due in 30 or 45 days? Why is this? Banks and mortgage companies will lead you to believe that they are doing you a favor because they know you have a lot of closing costs and moving expenses. Don't believe for a minute that they are doing you any favors. It's all about money to them. You may have heard the statement that interest on mortgages is paid in arrears, whereas rent is paid in advance. When you learn how much interest you are really paying, you will know what the term "in the rears" means. Unless there is a penalty clause for prepayment in your mortgage, which is stated in the note and mortgage instrument you signed, there is no compelling legal reason why you have to wait 30 to 45 days to make your first mortgage payment.

Make your first mortgage payment on the day of closing, and there is no interest due that can be charged for the first payment. Therefore, ALL of your first payment is paid against the principal, and none of the payment is paid in interest. You have to make the first payment anyway, so you should get in the habit of paying it early. But, what difference does this make?

If you pay your first payment at closing, then, your next monthly payment is amortizing a principal amount that is equal to one month's mortgage payment less than the stated principal amount of the note. Depending upon the amount of the mortgage, the interest rate, and the length of the mortgage, the savings could be equal to six or seven monthly payments and anywhere from $5,000 to $10,000 on your mortgage balance. The next time you attend a closing where you are financing or refinancing real estate, make the first payment at closing. The closing agent might protest that he cannot take your payment, or that it is not yet due, but insist upon your right to prepay.

If he insists, have the closing agent show you in the closing documents, which you signed, where there is a prepayment penalty. Make sure that your real estate note and mortgage do not have such a prepayment penalty. If it does, I would suggest that you get a different type loan. Also, make absolutely certain that your entire payment is applied against the principal and not to interest, or applied to the end of your loan or to your escrow account. Verify this with the mortgage company. Clearly indicate on your check that all of the payment is for principal only.

Let's look at a graphic example of this technique. We will be using the example of an $185,000 loan, at 7% interest, amortized over 30 years (360 months) with payments of $1,230.81.

| N (Number of Payments) | I/Y (Interest Rate) | PV (Amount of Loan) | PMT (Payment) |
|---|---|---|---|
| 360 | 7 | -185,000 | 1,230.81 |

If we apply the first payment of $1,230.81 to the original loan of $185,000, all of the payment goes to principal, which leaves a principal balance of $183,769.19.

| N (Number of Months Re-maining) | I/Y (Interest Rate) | PV (Amount of Loan) | PMT (Payment) |
|---|---|---|---|
| 352.05 | 7 | -183,769.19 | 1,230.81 |

You just saved a total of 7.95 months of payments or $9,784.94, and it didn't cost a dime. You just paid your closing costs and maybe your moving expenses, too! The higher the interest rate on your loan, and the higher the loan amount, the greater the savings.

To illustrate the power of compounding, what would be the result if you had applied the 7.95 months of payments you just saved to the principal up front at closing? That is, what would be the result of applying the $9,784.94 against the principal of the loan up front? It would reduce the loan amount to $175,215.06, and would save 54.93 payments, the equivalent of $67,608.36 in mortgage costs.

What happens if you didn't make your mortgage payment on the day of closing, but made an extra payment later, say on the 281$^{st}$ payment? If you made an extra payment on the 281$^{st}$ month, your loan balance would be $169,837.26. The number of payments would be reduced to 275.93 months, a savings of 5.07 months or $6,240.20. So the sooner you make the extra payments, the more you will save.

House Loan: $185,000
Interest Rate: 7.0%
Term: 30 years
Payment: $1,230.81

If first payment is paid at closing:
Number of payments remaining: 352.05
Total money saved: $9,784.94

If extra payment of $1,230.81 is paid on the 281$^{st}$ payment:
Number of months saved: 5.07 months
Amount saved: $6,240.20

# Notes:

# Technique #2

## Pay up front while it's cheap.
## This technique will save you one year of payments.

Take Technique #1 a step further. Why not pay a full years' principal on the day of closing? This will require just a little bit more investment up front, but will be well worth it. In the previous example, the first year's principal is $1,842.02. By making this payment at closing you will save a year of payments equivalent to $10,791.96 principal, or a total of $14,769.72 principal and interest. This will reduce the number of months on your loan from 360 months to 348 months, and a savings of $10,791.96 principal.

Why don't the banks and mortgage companies explain this to you? How long will it take you to amortize $1,842.02 principal the regular way? Maybe Congress should consider requiring this disclosure in the truth in lending laws. Millions of homeowners and real estate investors are over paying billions of dollars on their mortgages because of this "simple little matter of interest kicking you in the arrears." Refer to Appendix "A" for a sample letter to use when you send in an extra mortgage payment(s).

House Loan: $185,000
Interest Rate: 7.0%
Term: 30 years
Payment: $1,230.81
If one year's principal of $1,842.02 is paid at closing;

Number of payments saved: 12
Amount saved: $14,769.72

# Notes:

# Technique #3

## When you pay is as important as how much you pay. Save an average of 7 to 9 years.

If you pay your mortgage payments on a monthly basis like most people, it will cost you nearly twice the original purchase price of your home, assuming you make your payments over a thirty-year period, and on time. For example, if you purchased your home for $187,500, with a $150,000 mortgage (80%) and interest at 6% for 30 years and monthly payments of $899.33 per month, you will have paid $323,757.28. This is over twice the purchase price. You will have paid $173,757.28 in interest. This is more than the original purchase price in interest alone. Interest accrues while you sleep, 24 hours per day, seven days a week. If you are late on a payment, interest continues to accrue regardless of any late penalties you may pay.

Most mortgage payments are paid monthly. Paying your mortgage payments bi-weekly will have a dramatic effect on both the total amount you pay and the time it takes to pay off your mortgage. Most people are now familiar with the concept of bi-weekly mortgage payments even if they don't understand exactly how it works. Instead of making your payments on a monthly basis, you make one-half of your mortgage payment every two weeks. For example, if your mortgage payment of principal and interest were $850 per month, you would pay $425 every two weeks. This is equal to 13 monthly payments per year rather than 12. The extra monthly payment is applied to the remaining principal balance of the loan. The regular 30-year mortgage equals payments of $323,757 as opposed to bi weekly payments of $286,539, a difference of $37,218.

The higher the loan balance you have or the greater the interest rate, the larger the savings. This method is an excellent way for individuals who want to pay off their 30-year mortgages 7 to 8 years earlier, but who do not qualify for a 15-year mortgage. If you chose to purchase one of the many programs on the market offering "bi-weekly" mortgages, be careful you are getting a true bi-weekly mortgage program. Likewise, if you choose to pay on a bi-weekly basis, be sure you are really paying every two weeks and not twice a month. There is a difference.

Semi-monthly or twice a month means you are paying payments on the first and fifteenth of each month. This is calculated by taking the monthly payment of principal and interest and dividing it in half, and making two payments each month. There will be a total of 24 payments each year. There is a savings this way, but very little. You are paying down the principal quicker because you are making payments twice a month rather than once a month. True bi-weekly mortgage payments make quite a difference. If the payment is made every two weeks, then there are a total of 26 payments paid each year, or the equivalent of 13 monthly payments per year.

To calculate a true bi-weekly payment, take the monthly payment of principal and interest, divide it by 2, and multiply it by 26 (every two weeks). By utilizing this method of calculation, you will be saving money on interest payments and reducing the amortizing period.

Many homeowners and investors ask, "Why can't I just add principal payments to my regular payments?" You can, but most people don't. Make sure if you elect to do this, that the mortgage company applies the extra principal payment to the principal on the front end of the mortgage, and not to interest or to payments at the end of your mortgage, or even worse to your escrow account.

The way to calculate the amount to be paid on a true bi-weekly schedule is to take your monthly mortgage payment of principal and interest, divide it by 12, and pay that amount in a separate check to your mortgage company. Clearly indicate on the additional check that it is for additional principal. This technique will reduce your 30-year mortgage the same way as a bi-weekly mortgage plan, which you won't need to purchase from a bank or another source.

Be careful of the banks and mortgage companies that try to sell you their own bi-weekly mortgage plans. They will charge anywhere from $200 to $400 to set up their program, and a transfer fee of $2.50 to $6.95 every time a payment is moved from your checking account.

House Loan: $150,000
Interest Rate: 6.0%
Term: 30 years
Payment: Bi-weekly payments of $449.67
Total interest saved: $37,218.01
Months saved: 66

# Notes:

_____

_____

_____

_____

_____

_____

_____

_____

_____

# Notes:

# Technique #4

## Create your own adjustable payment mortgage.

If you want to determine how much you would have to increase your mortgage payment each month to pay off your mortgage in a certain period of time, take your financial calculator and under the number of payments put the number (N) of payments you would like to pay to eliminate your mortgage, and then recalculate for payment. For example, if you are currently paying on a $150,000 mortgage at 6% interest over 30 years, and you would like to pay it off in say 10 years, put 120 under the N on the calculator and calculate for payment. Go to: http://how-to-pay-off-mortgage-early.com and the software will calculate this for you.

| N | I/Y | PV | PMT | FV |
|---|-----|-----|-----|-----|
| 360 | 6 | 150,000 | 899.33 (Regular Payment) | 0 |

| N | I/Y | PV | PMT | FV |
|---|-----|-----|-----|-----|
| 120 | 6 | 150,000 | 1,665.31 (New Payment) | 0 |

The new payment necessary to pay off the above mortgage in 10 years rather than 30 years would be $1,665.31. The key is to pay as much principal as possible as early into the loan as possible.

# Notes:

# Technique #5

## Paying just a little bit more pays big dividends.

This is my favorite and the least painful way to pay off your mortgage fast. It is a very easy way to cut your amortization in half. First, obtain an amortization schedule of your current mortgage. Each month when you make your normal payment, send an additional check for the next month's principal. Make sure you clearly indicate on this additional check that it is for additional principal. Utilizing this method will cut your amortization exactly in half. That is, a 30-year mortgage will be fully paid in 15 years; a 20-year mortgage will paid off in 10 years, etc.

For each principal payment you make in advance, you are saving a full monthly mortgage payment of principal and interest. "More sooner is better," as the old saying goes.

Let's look at the savings on a $150,000 mortgage, payable over 30 years at 6% interest:

| N | I/Y | PV | PMT | FV |
|---|-----|-----|------|-----|
| 360 | 6 | 150,000 | 899.33 | 0 |

If you paid the next month's principal in advance, you would save 180 payments, or 180 payments x $899.33 monthly payment = $161,878.64.

The regular scheduled amortization of this loan would require you to make 250 monthly payments for 20.83 years before you reduce the principal to $75,949.68 (approximately half). There would be 110 payments of $899.33 remaining, or $98,926.30 still left to pay if you continued to pay your regular monthly payments.

# Notes:

# Technique #6

## Reverse compounding.

This technique requires discipline and good credit. However, it is effective, quick, and builds equity rapidly. The principle behind reverse compounding is the interruption of the compounding effect of the time value of money.

Making large payments of principal on a mortgage causes a dramatic reduction in the interest paid, and a subsequent rapid increase in equity buildup. This technique appears complicated at first glance, but is relatively easy to implement once all the elements are in place. There is no need to pay $3,500 or invest in some multi-level scheme to utilize this technique. You can do it on your own.

The first requirement is to obtain a line of credit, either a personal line of credit (LOC) or a home equity line of credit (HELOC). A HELOC is easier to obtain if the property has sufficient equity. If one has a rental property with a good cash flow and a large amount of equity, it is much easier to obtain a HELOC. Try to obtain a LOC or a HELOC at an interest rate of at least equal to or less than the interest rate on the mortgage you are going to pay off.

The second requirement is to obtain a free and clear credit card sufficient to pay all of your monthly living expenses, including your regular mortgage payment. You want to obtain one that has cash advance privileges, letting you obtain cash from an ATM machine when needed.

The credit card **must** be free and clear, and you must pay off the **entire monthly balance** each month. There are several considerations when selecting the credit card. First, the interest rate should be as low as possible. Otherwise, you will be defeating the whole principle of reverse compounding. Second, the billing cycle should contain the longest grace period possible. It should be no less than 25 days, and preferably 30 days. A word of caution is in order.

**DO NOT USE** a credit card that computes the interest rate based on the "average daily balance." Finally, select a credit card that has no annual fee.

There are several important points to consider before we get started in the mechanics of how reverse compounding works. First, make sure the mortgage you are paying off has no prepayment penalty. This can be determined by reading the mortgage note you signed and the recorded security instrument (mortgage, trust deed, or security deed).

When you make large advances toward the principal of your mortgage, always specify on the check and in a letter to the mortgage company that the payment is for additional principal. Clearly mark on the check that the entire payment is for principal. Always use a separate check when making additional principal payments. Finally, verify that the extra principal payment is applied to the front end of the principal balance and not the back end, or worse still, to your escrow account. Money put into your escrow account is worthless because it is not applied toward your mortgage payment. **Verify, Verify, Verify.**

Now let's get to the mechanics. Let's use the example of a $200,000 mortgage payable over 30 years (360 payments) with an interest rate of 6% and payments of $1,199.10 per month. It appears as follows on the financial calculator.

| N | I/Y | PV | PMT | FV |
|---|---|---|---|---|
| 360 | 6 | -200,000 | 1,199.10 | 0 |

Let's assume further that you have been able to obtain a home equity line of credit of $30,000 based upon the appraised value of your home of $250,000. Let's further assume that your net take home income is $8,000 per month and that your monthly expenses including your regular mortgage payment are $7,000 per month. You have obtained a credit card with a credit limit of $10,000, and it has a zero balance.

**Step 1:** Determine how much principal you wish to pay against your mortgage. If you want to make advance principal payments every 6 months, the following formula is beneficial. Take your surplus monthly income over expenses and multiply that amount times 5, and then add back your monthly income. For example:

SURPLUS INCOME ($1,000 month) x 5 + MONTHLY INCOME ($8,000) = $13,000 (amount to pay on mortgage) every six months

**Step 2:** After you have determined the amount you wish to pay against your mortgage (in this case, $13,000), pay this amount out of your HELOC or LOC to your mortgage company as principal against your mortgage. Keep the remaining $17,000 of your HELOC or LOC as reserve.

**Step 3:** Pay all of your monthly living expenses with your new free and clear credit card ($7,000 in our example).

**Step 4:** Use your monthly income ($8,000 in our example) to pay back your HELOC or LOC. This will leave a balance owing on your HELOC or LOC of $5,000 and a debt of $7,000 on your credit card.

**Step 5:** Next month, during the grace period, pay your credit card in full with your HELOC or LOC. This leaves a zero balance on your credit card, but a $13,000 balance on your HELOC or LOC. This $13,000 balance is created by the $7,000 used to pay off your credit card and the $5,000 balance on your HELOC or LOC.

**Step 6:** Pay your new monthly expenses of $7,000 with the credit card. Put your net monthly check of $8,000 into your HELOC or LOC account. After your monthly expenses are paid there will be $1,000 left over from your income. Pay this against your HELOC or LOC. Repeat these steps for the next 13 months and your HELOC or LOC will be paid off.

**Step 7:** Repeat these steps and pay another $13,000 towards your mortgage from your HELOC or LOC. Continue to do this until your mortgage is paid in full.

# Notes:

_____

_____

_____

_____

_____

_____

_____

_____

_____

_____

_____

# Technique #7

## Use a credit card to pay off mortgage.

Is it really possible to pay your mortgage off with a credit card? The answer is yes! And did you know that it is less expensive than the regular method of paying your mortgage? But how is this possible? Credit card companies charge high rates, sometimes as high as 30%. The secret lies in the magic of daily compounding.

Let's take the example of a 30 year, $125,000 mortgage at 7.5% interest, and payments of $874.02.

Normal Method: 30 year fixed rate mortgage at 7.5% for $125,000.

| N | I/Y | PV | PMT | FV |
|---|-----|-----|------|-----|
| 360 | 7.5 | -125,000 | 874.02 | 0 |

At the end of 3 years, you will have paid $3,732.19 principal and $27,732.46 interest for a total of $31,464.65.

Loan balance at end of 3 years = $121,267.81

What would be the result if you used a credit card instead?

Use credit card Instead: 36 months, 19% interest and pay 10% of principal ($12,500)

| N | I/Y | PV | PMT | FV |
|---|-----|-----|------|-----|
| 36 | 19 | -12,500 | 458.20 | 0 |

Cost of using credit card is $458.20 x 36 = $16,495.21 (borrow $12,500 on credit card and apply to mortgage)

Cost of regular mortgage is $874.02 x 36 = $31,464.72

Difference in loan balances: $121,267.81- normal mortgage
$112,500.00- credit card
------------------------------------
$8,767.81 – principal difference paid

It requires 98.05 months to reduce the above mortgage to a balance of $112,500, using the normal method of paying a mortgage.

What if you didn't have the cash to make the credit card payments each month? If you have several credit cards and/or a HELOC (home equity line of credit), you can follow the procedure similar to the one that follows:

1. Borrow $12,500 from your American Express card, and pay this amount against the principal of your mortgage.

2. Next month, before the interest is due, borrow $12,500 from your Visa or Master Card, and pay back American Express.

3. The next month, before the interest is due, borrow $12,500 from your HELOC or other credit card and pay back your Visa.

4. Repeat this procedure every month. You have just created an interest free loan.

Use any surplus monthly income or tax refunds to pay off your credit cards as they become due. If it takes you 3 years to pay off your credit cards, you are still saving a tremendous amount of money over your normal method of amortization.

After you have paid off your credit cards, repeat the process.

Take your tax refund generated by the interest tax deduction and apply it to the credit card debt (3 years).

If you had paid the same principal amount ($3,732.19) using a credit card at 19% (with a monthly payment of $874.02), it would take 4.46 months rather than amortizing the mortgage debt for 36 months at 7.5%. That is, 36 payments on the mortgage at $874.02 per month cost $31,464.72 to reduce the principal by $3,732.19. Using a credit card at 19% interest, it costs $3,898.13, a difference of $27,566.59.

House Loan: $125,000.00
Interest Rate: 7.5%
Term: 30 years
Monthly payment: $874.02

It costs $14,285.24 and 16.34 months to reduce the principal balance of this mortgage to $112,500 using a credit card. It requires 98 months to reduce the principal balance of this mortgage to $112,509.08, using the normal amortization at a cost of $85,697.48

Savings by using credit card: $71,412.24

# Notes:

_____

_____

_____

_____

_____

_____

# Notes:

# Technique #8

## The Full Monte.

"I am up to my eyeballs in debt, I am sinking fast, and I can't afford to pay another dime on my mortgage," you exclaim. Foreclosures are at an all time high. Millions are losing their homes in foreclosures in record numbers. The sub-prime loan business is a train wreck, and the adjustable rate mortgage scheme has proven to be a disaster.

The enemy, my friend, is DEBT. Whether it is in the form of a mortgage payment or a credit card payment, when you owe money to someone else you are a slave, a debtor, working for someone else (creditors), and in bondage. My native state of Georgia was founded as a haven from the debtor's prisons of England. Maybe this is why I am so passionate about debt elimination.

There are others who have preceded me in this arena for many more years than I have been an advocate. I have chosen to focus on real estate debt because I have had more experience with it throughout my professional career. My hat goes off to those others who have blazed the trail before me. Their techniques work. They are not complicated, but they are not easy.

If you do not have the extra cash needed to utilize my preceding techniques, I suggest that you adopt the following plan. It is simple, but requires absolute discipline. The plan is as follows:

1. List all your debts in the order of the smallest balances first. Don't worry about the interest rates. If the balances are about the same, pay the debts with the highest interest rates first.

2. Pay the minimum payments required on all your other debts until you have completely paid off the debt with the lowest balance.

3. After the debt with the lowest balance is paid, repeat the process, and apply all the extra income that you were paying on the previous debt to the debt with the next lowest balance.

4. Repeat this process until all your debts are paid except your mortgage.

All your debts are now paid except your mortgage. At this point, ATTACK, ATTACK, ATTACK! Apply all the money you were formerly paying on your other debts to your mortgage payment.

How long will it take to pay off my mortgage, you ask? Suppose it took you eleven months to pay off your other debts. You still have not even dented the principal balance of your mortgage if you have been making your regular payments as scheduled.

For example, let's say you have a relatively new 30-year mortgage with the original principal balance of $185,000. Your interest rate is 6%, and your payments are $1,109.17 per month. You have made eleven regular payments on your mortgage, and your loan balance is $182,922.73.

Since you have paid off all your debts, you have an extra $3,000 per month to apply against your mortgage. Add the $3,000 together with the $1,109.17 regular mortgage payment, and you will now be paying $4,109.17 per month toward your mortgage payment. Here is how it appears on the financial calculator:

## REGULAR METHOD

| N | I/Y | PV | PMT | FV |
|---|---|---|---|---|
| 349 | 6 | -182,922.73 | 1,109.17 | 0 |

## ACCELERATED METHOD

| N | I/Y | PV | PMT | FV |
|---|---|---|---|---|
| 50.48 | 6 | -182,922.73 | 4,109.17 | 0 |

Are you kidding me?  My mortgage will be paid off in 50.48 months (4.21 years)?  That's right, my friend.  Now you are completely debt free, including your mortgage, in a total of 61.48 months (5.12 years).

In addition to the interest payments you have eliminated on your other debts, you have eliminated 298.52 mortgage payments, and a total of $331,109.43 in mortgage debt.

After you have walked across your paid for grass for a few days, take a vacation.  Pay cash.  And, put the rest of those wasted interest payments in an investment program that pays you and not the mortgage company.  You are now free at last.

Loan Balance: $182,922.73
Interest Rate: 6.0%
Original Term: 30 years
Original Monthly Payment: $1,109.17
Accelerated Payoff:  $4,109.17
Term: 50.48 months
Amount Saved; $331,109.43

# Notes:

# Technique #9

## Beat the ARM - taking the adjustment out of the Adjustable Rate Mortgage.

The best way to beat the adjustable rate mortgage is to refinance and get into a fixed rate mortgage. The adjustable rate mortgage is designed to benefit the bank and not the mortgage payer.

If it is not possible to refinance, or if you can't qualify without horrendous refinancing costs that will eat up the equity in your home, you might consider the following technique. It is a modification of Technique #8, "The Full Monte", but works the same way, with one exception. Instead of paying off your other indebtedness first and your mortgage last, you will be attacking your mortgage first, at least until the first adjustment on your ARM.

You will be making the extra payments on your mortgage until the first adjustment occurs. This means that your payment will not increase. The reason for this modification from Technique #8 is to prevent the occurrence of anymore outgoing cash flow.

After this is achieved, you might want to go back to Technique #8, and pay off all your other debts, and then finish paying off the balance of your mortgage.

Let's look at an example: Your mortgage balance is $150,000, payable over 30 years (360 months) with an initial interest rate of 6%, and payments of $899.33. The note and mortgage provide *"that the payment will not adjust during the first two years of the loan, and will not increase by more than 3 percentage points. The mortgage will adjust every 6 months thereafter, based on the current LIBOR rate plus the margin stated in the note."*

What does all this mean? It means that the mortgage payment could increase from $899.33 per month up to $1193.45 per month, a $294.12 increase. This plays havoc for anyone who has dreams of paying off his mortgage in his lifetime. It also increases the risk of default and wrecks the family budget.

Let's go back to our technique. We need to pay down the principal balance enough in two years to prevent an increase in the payment so there will be no increase in the payment in two years. We will then be able to apply any extra cash flow to our indebtedness. If you made your regular mortgage payments for two years, the loan balance would be $146,202.35. But, now your mortgage has an adjustment due which could increase your payment to $1,193.45 per month from $899.33 per month.

The question is: How much principal must you pay in 24 months to prevent an increase in your payment, based on the maximum adjustment increase? The answer is $38,229.59. You must reduce your loan balance in 24 months from $150,000 to $111,770.41. This will require you to pay an additional $1,592.90 per month on your mortgage payment to prevent an increase in your mortgage payment in two years, or you should utilize some or all of the previous techniques.

This is the reason you might consider applying your extra income to your mortgage payment rather than to your other debts for the first two years of your mortgage. It appears as follows on the financial calculator.

### PRESENT MORTGAGE:

| N | I/Y | PV | PMT | FV |
|---|-----|----|----|----|
| 360 | 6 | -150,000 | 899.33 | 0 |

### BALANCE AFTER TWO YEARS AND BEFORE ADJUSTMENT:

| N | I/Y | PV | PMT | FV |
|---|-----|----|----|----|
| 336 | 6 | -146,202.35 | 899.33 | 0 |

## PAYMENT AFTER ADJUSTMENT:

| N | I/Y | PV | PMT | FV |
|---|-----|-----|-----|-----|
| 336 | 9 | -146,202.35 | 1,193.45 | 0 |

### ADD $1,592.90 PER MONTH TO MORTGAGE PAYMENT:

### BALANCE AFTER 24 MONTHS

| N | I/Y | PV | PMT | FV |
|---|-----|-----|-----|-----|
| 360 | 6 | -105,691.68 | 2,492.23 | 0 |

## MORTGAGE PAYMENT AFTER ADJUSTMENT AND RATE INCREASE:

| N | I/Y | PV | PMT | FV |
|---|-----|-----|-----|-----|
| 336 | 9 | -105,691.68 | 862.76 | 0 |

You now see how expensive adjustable rate mortgages are. You now have two choices. You can revert to Technique # 8, and pay off your other debts, and then pay off the balance of your mortgage. Or you can continue making the extra payments on your mortgage and pay it off first. The choice is yours. Look at the terms of the ARM and make the determination of which choice is more advantageous to you. If you pay off your other debts first, you will have more money to pay off your mortgage sooner. The choice is yours.

> House Loan: $150,000
> Interest Rate: 6.0%
> Term: 30 years
> Loan balance at the end of 24 months- The 1st adjustment on ARM Mortgage – $146,202.25
>
> By paying an additional $1,592.90 per month for 24 months the payment remains the same after the ARM adjustment.

# What side of the mortgage do you want do be on?

When you invest in income producing property, where does most of the rental income go? Most of the rental income stream goes right back to the lender that lent you the money to buy the property in the first place, plus interest, of course. For example, suppose you find a great bargain, a house that is valued at $250,000, which can be purchased for $150,000 through a foreclosure, short sale, subject to, or some other means of acquiring a bargain investment property. You locate a lender that makes investment property loans at 80% loan to value at 9% interest with three discount points plus closing costs.

You obtain the new 80% loan on the property for $200,000 at 9% interest for 180 months, with a balloon payment in 10 years, and payments of $2,028.53 and $7,500 in discount points and closing costs. Over the 10-year period, assuming you keep the property that long, you will have spent $372,635.97 in financing costs, not to mention taxes, insurance, repairs, and the other costs associated with ownership. This will, of course, be offset by any rental income you receive plus income tax write offs. It will take a lot of rent and tax write-off in order to overcome the financing costs. The point is, "your bargain" has been eaten alive by the mortgage alligator.

You collect the money from the tenant. You plunge the toilets. You chase and dispossess the tenants who won't pay. In addition, you also take the risk of negative cash flow, damage, destruction, devaluation, and vacancies. If you have a tenant, you have no collateral for your payment. You are loaning him money to live in your property, specifically because he cannot afford to own it. A tenant is not an owner, and pride of ownership is not there. In an economic decline, a landlord's equity can be eliminated by a drop in property values.

Wouldn't you rather be the bank? When you invest in "paper," you become the bank. You, as a lender, have fixed payments and costs. The lender's equity takes priority. If the fair market of the property or the rent goes down, the payments on the mortgages are fixed.

When real estate values increase, mortgages can increase in value too. When property values go up, owners refinance more frequently. When the payers of the mortgage, which you own, refinance, they pay you off in full for the full value of the notes. Your yield increases dramatically.

For example, if you purchase a mortgage with a face value of $25,000 for $19,000, the mortgage could be paid off overnight at full face value, and a profit of $6,000. In addition, when a payer of a note increases his payment, the yield could double. The leverage possibilities of notes can exceed all other investments.

# How to receive rather than pay on a mortgage.

**"It's more blessed to receive than to give."**

There are many reasons why one would choose to finance the real estate he just sold. Ordinarily a buyer would go to a bank or mortgage company and get a loan. Title to the property is transferred at closing, and the seller gets his money. The buyer pays each month for usually up to thirty years. However, there are times when property is sold without commercial lending involvement. The purchaser might not be able to qualify for a traditional loan. The property might be the type on which it is difficult to obtain traditional financing, such as undeveloped property or over- improved property. On the other hand, the seller might be inflexible, and is not willing to negotiate on selling price.

In these instances, the properties might be sold with "owner carry back" financing. The seller now becomes the bank and makes the profit.

# It works like this:

Sam Seller has an over- improved property located in a nice middle class neighborhood. Sam is inflexible on the price. It is valued at $250,000. The houses in the neighborhood are valued at $150,000. However, Sam is willing to owner finance the property at 8% interest for 20 years if the buyer will put 10% down.

Billy Buyer has $25,000 he can use as a down payment, but he cannot qualify for a mortgage because he owes too much on credit cards, student loans, and he has only been employed for six months. He is a young dentist just out of dental school. His prospects for good income are promising. Billy's new bride just loves Sam's house, and is already arranging the furniture in her mind. The parties reach an agreement. Billy and his bride Barbara will buy the house at the full asking price of $250,000. They will put $25,000 down. Sam Seller will finance the balance of $225,000 at 8% interest for 20 years with payments of $1,881.58 per month. The closing will take place in 30 days.

The closing takes place as scheduled. Now, Sam becomes the banker. Sam received his full asking price, but he will have to wait 20 years to get all his money.

## How to make money from somebody else's mortgage.

Can Sam sell his mortgage to an investor? Yes, **you** as an investor can make money buying Sam's newly created mortgage, but not for its full face value. You will want to buy Sam's mortgage at a discount. As we have learned, today's dollars are worth more than future dollars. The dollars Sam collects today are worth far more than the dollars he collects over a 20-year period.

Sam agrees to sell us his mortgage for a discount, but he does not want to sell it for the $135,273 it would take to give you a 16% yield. So, you offer to buy the next 60 payments for $56,250, or one-fourth (1/4) of the mortgage for the next one-fourth (1/4) of the remaining principal balance. This appears to be a win-win situation for all the parties. There appears to be no discount to Sam. Sam obviously does not understand the principles of the time value of money.

You run the numbers through your financial calculator and they appear as follows:

| N | I/Y | PV | PMT | FV |
|---|---|---|---|---|
| 240 | 8 | -225,000 | 1,881.99 | 0-Original Loan |

| N | I/Y | PV | PMT | FV |
|---|---|---|---|---|
| 60 | 31.78 | -56,250 | 1,881.99 | 0-Sell ¼ Note |

Your yield turns out to be a whopping 31.78%. Sam gets a lump sum of $56,250 for the next 60 payments (1/4 of the principal balance of the mortgage), and in exchange, you get to collect the next 60 payments. You will be collecting $112,919.41 worth of payments for an investment of $56,250.

# How it works:

Suppose you bought a house for $200,000 and you rented it for $1,500 per month. Your yearly income would be $18,000 on an investment of $200,000. Your return would be 9%. (the $18,000 annual income divided by the $200,000 investment). If you could purchase the identical house for half the price ($100,000), and the rental income remained the same ($18,000), your return would double to 18%.

The basic concept is this: If you invest in an income producing asset such a rental property or "paper," the less we pay for it, the greater our return if the income produced by that asset remains the same.

# What is paper?

When you buy real estate, you sign a document at the closing called the promissory note, which is the instrument that spells out the terms of repayment of the money you borrowed to buy the real estate. The promissory note provides the amount owed, to whom it is to be paid, the interest rate, the terms of repayment, and the person or persons who are obligated to repay the debt. The promissory note is rarely recorded in the deed records.

The other instrument, which you will sign, is a security instrument called the mortgage, security deed, or deed of trust. The type of security instrument varies from state to state, and the procedures of default and foreclosure vary from state to state. The type of instrument used, and the default and foreclosure procedures are governed by state and not federal laws.

This instrument secures the promissory note, and creates a lien or encumbrance against the real estate. It is almost always recorded in the deed records in the county where the property is located.

"Paper" is the term used in the cash flow business, which usually means a promissory note (I owe you), secured by a mortgage, security deed, or deed of trust on real estate. "Paper" is also a term that is used to describe options, leaseholds, land contracts, and other cash flow producing assets. The term "seller- carry back mortgage" is used when the seller of real estate holds or "carries back" the mortgage, security deed, or deed of trust. The seller of the property is like the bank. He holds or "carries back" the mortgage in lieu of receiving the full purchase price today. The seller of the property has elected to receive a cash flow (payments) over a period of time (N) in lieu of cash. That cash flow is the time related return of principal (PV) over a specified period (N).

When an investor purchases the income stream with cash dollars today for future dollars to be received, a discount occurs. Discounting is the reverse of compounding. The cash dollar value of a future cash flow is realized when the "paper" is purchased at a discount.

Interest and yield are not the same even though the numbers can be the same. Interest is a percentage that a lender charges for the use of his money. Yield, on the other hand, is the amount of the profit divided by the amount of money invested. Yield is often called the "return on investment."

The difference between interest and yield can be explained as follows.

**Example 1:**  If an investor is receiving 12% simple annual interest on a $15,000 note due in one year, then the investor receives a total of $1,800 interest plus his principal of $15,000 for a total of $16,800.  The yield is determined by dividing the amount of profit by the amount invested.  The $1,800 profit is divided by the $15,000 invested.  The yield is 12%.  The investor's return on investment or the yield is 12%.

**Example 2:** If the investor needed some money sooner than one year, he could sell the $15,000 note at a discount.  If he needed $10,000 immediately, he could sell the note at a $5,000 discount.  What is the note buyer's return on investment or the yield?

In order to determine the note buyer's yield, determine all the profit the note buyer will earn, and then divide the profit by the purchase price of the note.  The note buyer paid $10,000 for the note that has a face value of $15,000.  The $5,000 discount is part of the profit.

In addition to the $5,000 discount, the note buyer will receive $1,800 in interest when the note is due in 12 months.  Add the $5,000 discount together with the $1,800 interest received for a total profit of $6,800.  Divide the total profit ($6,800) by the amount the note buyer invested ($10,000) and the return on investment or the yield is 68%.

The faster the dollars are received, the higher the yield.  Conversely, the longer one waits to receive the payments, the lower the yield.

"Yield to maturity" is defined as the overall rate of return on an investment if one holds the "paper" to maturity, and includes the normal "yield" as a component, as well as the financed rate of return from any balloon payments received.

# Notes:

# Technique #10

## Invest in your own debt.

### Buying Your Debt at a Discount Will Get You Out Of Debt Quicker.

The remaining techniques are more creative in their application of the time value of money, and are primarily utilized by those who have owner financed mortgages and by real estate investors.

The best investment you can make is to invest in your own debt. You will increase the yields on your money, and you will reach financial freedom quicker by eliminating the monthly outgo of payments to creditors. It is highly recommended that you develop a plan to eliminate all of your debts, starting with your credit cards. By doing this, you will advance steadily toward financial freedom, and have more funds to apply against your mortgage indebtedness.

If you are currently paying on an owner-financed mortgage, offer to purchase a percentage of the outstanding indebtedness for that same percentage of payments. For example, offer to purchase one fourth of the remaining payments of your mortgage for one fourth of the remaining principal balance.

To illustrate, if you owe a mortgage with a principal balance of $100,000, and an interest rate of 8% with a term of 10 years, offer to buy $25,000 of the principal balance mortgage for the next 30 payments. This offer is made to the person you are making your payments to each month. On the financial calculator, it looks like this:

| N | I/Y | PV | PMT | FV |
|-----|-------|----------|----------|----------------------|
| 120 | 8 | -100,000 | 1,213.28 | 0-Original mortgage |

| N | I/Y | PV | PMT | FV |
|----|-------|---------|----------|----------------------|
| 30 | 31.41 | -25,000 | 1,213.28 | 0-Partial purchase |

This creates a 31.41% return on your investment! You say, that is great, but I don't have $25,000 to purchase my mortgage. If you don't have it, somebody else does. Find an investor or an institutional investor who will buy the payments at a lesser yield, say for 12%, and split the remaining profit with them.

What would the profit be if you bought 30 payments (one fourth of the mortgage) for $25,000 (one fourth of the loan balance), then turned around, and sold these same payments for a yield of 12%? It would look like this on the financial calculator:

| N | I/Y | PV | PMT | FV |
|---|---|---|---|---|
| 30 | 31.41 | -25,000 | 1,213.28 | 0 payments purchased |

| N | I/Y | PV | PMT | FV |
|---|---|---|---|---|
| 30 | 12 | -31,311.87 | 1,213.28 | 0 payments purchased |

You would be buying your own debt for $25,000 and selling it for $31,311.87 for a profit of $6,311.87. This would create enough extra cash to make 5.20 monthly payments. For someone in financial distress and facing foreclosure, would not this buy some time to straighten out the financial dilemma?

Let's take this one-step further. Suppose you sold your debt to an investor, and made a profit of $6,311.87. Then, if you applied the $6,311.87 to the principal balance of your loan (assuming a loan balance of $100,000), you would reduce your principal balance to $93,688.13, thereby saving 11.16 payments or $13,540.16. Do you not think that the mortgagee (owner financer) would be impressed with the fact that you paid him an additional $6,311.87 toward your mortgage?

# Technique #11

## Buy high, sell low.

Is this a typographical error? Can anybody really make a profit by buying high and selling low? You can when we are talking about interest rates. If you are facing financial difficulties or you just want to save money on your mortgage payments, try this technique. If you are currently paying on a seller-financed mortgage, offer to pay the next 12 mortgage payments in advance. If you pay in advance, ask for a discount. Start with 20% and maybe you can negotiate a 10% discount.

For example, if you are paying the seller a monthly payment of $899.33, offer to pay $8,633.57, for the next 12 payments ($899.33 x 12 months x .20 discount). It looks like this on the financial calculator:

| N | I/Y | PV | PMT | FV |
|---|-----|-----|------|-----|
| 12 | 43.34 | -8,633.57 | 899.33 | 0-Payments purchased |

You have just earned a 43.34% return for investing in your own mortgage payment. What if you don't have $8,633.57 to invest in your own mortgage? If you don't have it, somebody else does. Find an investor who wants to earn a 25% return on his money and sell him the payments. It appears like this on the financial calculator:

| N | I/Y | PV | PMT | FV |
|---|-----|-----|------|-----|
| 12 | 25 | -9,462.23 | 899.33 | 0-Payments purchased |

Your investor just made a 25% return on his money by buying 12 months of your mortgage payments. You just received $828.66 for selling your own debt. Your mortgage is paid 12 months in advance. Of course, you have to pay the investor $899.33 each month, but you reduced your mortgage payment $69.05 each month for the next 12 months. Repeat the process annually and let somebody else pay your mortgage payments at a discount.

Could you not do this utilizing income producing rental properties? A 20-year mortgage could be paid off in 3, 5, 7, or maybe 10 years sooner by utilizing this method. The next time you are making a payment on a seller financed property, think BUY HIGH, SELL LOW.

P.S. Try to get an agreement from your mortgage holder to allow you to do this annually.

# Notes:

---

---

---

---

---

---

---

---

# Technique #12

## Let somebody else's debt pay off the mortgage on your house or rental property.

### Put Your Mortgage on "Automatic Pilot Payoff".

There is a better way to pay off your mortgage than out of your own pocket, or from rent proceeds. Let somebody else's debt pay it for you. This technique requires some knowledge of investing in discounted notes and mortgages. Let's examine how this works. Your property has an appraised value of $300,000. There is an existing loan balance of $50,000, and you want to utilize the equity to make other investments.

Obtain a new mortgage for $240,000 (80% loan to value) at 6% interest, for 360 months and payments of $1438.92.

From the new loan proceeds of $240,000, pay off your old mortgage of $50,000, leaving a balance of $190,000. These proceeds are tax-free because it is borrowed money. Borrowed money is currently not taxable under the tax code.

Invest the $190,000 in a discounted mortgage or mortgages yielding at least 24%. Review the previous examples as to how this works. It appears like this on the financial calculator:

| N | I/Y | PV | PMT | FV |
|---|---|---|---|---|
| 120 | 24 | -190,000 | 4,189.14 | 0-Investment in discounted mortgage(s) |

In the example above, we invested the $190,000 loan proceeds from the new loan in a mortgage or combination of mortgages or partials of mortgages for 10 years (120 months) at a yield of 24%. The cash flow from this investment is $4,189.14 per month for the next 120 months. See our previous examples of how to obtain a 24 % return on your investment.

There is an income stream of $4,189.14 coming in each month for the next 120 months, but there is also a new mortgage payment of $1,438.92 for the next 360 months (30 years). It appears like this on the financial calculator:

| N | I/Y | PV | PMT | FV |
|---|---|---|---|---|
| 360 | 6 | -240,000 | 1,438.92 | 0-New loan |

Pay the $4,189.14 coming in from the discounted mortgages investment and apply the income to our new mortgage. It appears like this on the financial calculator:

| N | I/Y | PV | PMT | FV |
|---|---|---|---|---|
| 67.67 | 6 | -240,000 | 4,189.14 | 0-Additional payment on new loan |

The new loan of $240,000 is paid off in 67.67 months (5.64 years) instead of the scheduled 360 months (30 years). Now, somebody else's debt, is making the payments for you.

It gets better! There are 52.33 months left from the investment in the discounted mortgage(s). There are 52.33 months times $4,189.14 = $219,217.70 income coming in after our real estate mortgage is paid off.

In summary: The house is paid for in 5.64 years with someone else's money, and there is $219,217.70 left over. Albert Einstein was correct when he said that compound interest was the eighth wonder of the world.

This is an excellent technique if you have a property with a lot of equity with more than 5 years left to pay on your mortgage.

# Technique #13

## Pay the full asking price, receive a 44% discount, put money in your pocket at closing, have somebody else make 75% or the monthly payments, and pay your home off 20 years sooner.

One of the greatest real estate investment techniques known, called substitution of collateral, is the technique that causes many to look seriously at investing in discount notes and mortgages rather than real estate. The technique is best explained with an example. You have located an attractive real estate investment with an asking price of $300,000. It has just been appraised for that, so you don't even bother to negotiate the price. You offer to purchase it at the full asking price.

Since you are willing to pay the full asking price, the seller is willing to owner finance if you will agree to pay with a 20% down payment of $60,000. The owner is willing to finance $240,000 in the form of a first mortgage with 8% interest, 15 years (180 payments), and payments of $2,293.57 per month.

Since you are willing to pay the full purchase price on the owner's terms, she gives you another concession on the financing. You propose, and the seller agrees, to allow you to substitute the mortgage you were planning to give her on the property with a mortgage on another property of equal or greater value.

You locate a mortgage for sale at a discount on a property of equal or greater value. The mortgage has a loan balance of approximately $240,000, and has similar rates and terms as the mortgage you were going to give the seller. You option to purchase this mortgage at a 20% yield. The mortgage appears like this on the financial calculator.

| N | I/Y | PV | PMT | FV |
|---|---|---|---|---|
| 180 | 8 | -240,000 | 2,293.57 | 0-Mortgage to be purchased at a discount |

| N | I/Y | PV | PMT | FV |
|---|---|---|---|---|
| 180 | 20 | -130,590.99 | 2,293.57 | 0-Amount paid for discounted mortgage |

The second step is to obtain a new mortgage from a mortgage company or bank for $240,000 (80% LTV). Let's assume that you obtained a $240,000 mortgage for 30 years (360 months) at 6% interest with payments of $1,438.92. It appears like this on the financial calculator.

| N | I/Y | PV | PMT | FV |
|---|---|---|---|---|
| 360 | 6 | -240,000 | 1,438.92 | 0-New mortgage |

The third step is the closing. You exercise your option, and purchase the substitute mortgage on the other property for $130,590.99 using the new loan proceeds from the bank. Pay the $60,000 down payment to the seller of the property. This action leaves $49,409.01, which is the money left over. Use it anyway you desire. You might consider investing the $49,000 in another discounted note and paying the monthly cash flow on the new mortgage you just originated at the bank. For example, if you invested the $49,000 in a discounted mortgage at a yield of 24% for 10 years, it would appear like this on the financial calculator:

| N | I/Y | PV | PMT | FV |
|---|---|---|---|---|
| 120 | 24 | -49,000 | 1,080.36 | 0 |

If you paid the $1,080.36 derived from this mortgage in addition to your regular payment of $1,438.92, for a total of $2,520.28 per month, your mortgage will be fully paid in 129.63 months rather than 360 months. This is 19.20 years sooner, with a savings of $331,484.00 over the life of the mortgage.

In summary: The property was purchased for the full asking price at a 44% discount with 20% equity in the property from date of purchase. Someone else is making 75% of the monthly payment. You received $49,000 cash at closing, income tax free, and your house is paid off in a little over 10 years at a savings of $331,383.28 in mortgage payments.

# Notes:

_____

_____

_____

_____

_____

# Notes:

_____

_____

_____

_____

_____

_____

_____

_____

_____

_____

_____

# Technique #14

## Pay the full asking price, put money in your pocket at closing, never make a payment, and get paid every month without tenants.

This technique is a variation of Technique #13. Instead of obtaining bank financing to purchase the discounted mortgage, you can use the technique of partial mortgages. It is especially effective for investors who are not planning to hold a property more than 5 years.

Instead of purchasing the discounted mortgage that you would purchase in Technique #13, you would purchase 4 partials (part of a mortgage) on 4 separate mortgages. It is easier to get someone to accept your offer to purchase a part of a mortgage if you offer him the full price for part of a mortgage.

For example, if Fred has a 20-year, $240,000 mortgage at 8% interest, his payments would be $2007.46 per month. You would offer him $60,000 for the next 60 payments. It would look like the following on the financial calculator.

| N | I/Y | PV | PMT | FV |
|---|---|---|---|---|
| 240 | 8 | -240,000 | 2,007.46 | 0-Original note |

| N | I/Y | PV | PMT | FV |
|---|---|---|---|---|
| 60 | 31.78 | -60,000 | 2,007.46 | 0-Partial purchased |

By buying 60 monthly payments, or one-fourth of the mortgage, for one-fourth of the principal balance, creates a yield of 31.78%.

How does this work in buying a house? After you have optioned to purchase the partial mortgage from the note seller, sell the same partial to an investor or institutional buyer at a lesser yield, for example, 18%.

It would look like the following on the financial calculator.

| N | I/Y | PV | PMT | FV |
|---|---|---|---|---|
| 60 | 31.78 | -60,000 | 2,007.46 | 0-Partial bought |

| N | I/Y | PV | PMT | FV |
|---|---|---|---|---|
| 60 | 18 | -79,054.31 | 2,007.46 | 0-Partial sold to investor/institutional investor |

You can see that you just made a $19,054.31 profit from the sale of each partial you just bought.

How does this apply to your original purchase of the $300,000 home? If you purchased 4 partials for $60,000 each on different mortgages or similar mortgages, your profit would be $57,162.48 if you sold 3 of the 4 partials.

Offer $50,000 as your down payment, leaving a balance of $250,000 owed on the purchase price. It appears as follows on the financial calculator.

| N | I/Y | PV | PMT | FV |
|---|---|---|---|---|
| 360 | 8 | -250,000 | 1,834.41 | 0 |

Another technique would be to offer the seller of the house 40 payments on his mortgage, in advance, in lieu of a down payment. That is, offer him $73,376.40, representing 40 advance payments rather than the $50,000 down payment originally agreed upon.

By doing this, all $73,376.46 would be credited toward principal. It would look like this on the financial calculator:

| N | I/Y | PV | PMT | FV |
|---|---|---|---|---|
| 360 | 8 | -300,000 | 2,201.29 | 0-Before 40 payments made |

| N | I/Y | PV | PMT | FV |
|---|---|---|---|---|
| 174.49 | 8 | -226,623.54 | 2,201.20 | 0-After 40 payments made |

This would reduce the term of the mortgage from 360 months to 174.49 months, a reduction of 186 months (15.46 years) or a savings of $408,362 in mortgage payments. The choice is yours, whatever you can negotiate.

    New loan amount: $226,623.60
    Interest rate: 8.0%
    Term: 174 monthly payments
    Payment: $2,201.29
    Total amount saved: $408,362
    Months saved: 186

# Notes:

_____

_____

_____

_____

# Notes:

_____

_____

_____

_____

_____

_____

_____

_____

_____

_____

_____

_____

# Technique #15

## Piggyback your mortgage onto a larger mortgage for free.

This is a technique whereby a larger mortgage, which you purchase, pays off your home mortgage simultaneously. The better description would be having a partial mortgage pay off a full mortgage. It is a technique which incorporates the other techniques previously discussed.

For example, you locate a commercial or residential property with a $500,000 first mortgage with a 6% interest rate, which is amortized over 360 months with payments of $2,997.75. You purchase one year's worth of principal for $16,666.67 (no discount). It appears as follows on the financial calculator.

| N | I/Y | PV | PMT | FV |
|---|---|---|---|---|
| 360 | 6 | -500,000 | 2,997.75 | 0-The original loan |

| N | I/Y | PV | PMT | FV |
|---|---|---|---|---|
| 12 | 172.93 | -16,666.67 | 2,997.75 | One year's principal |

Offer either an investor or the note holder a 24% yield on his money for an investment of $16,666, for a period of one year, with an option for 10 more years. It appears as follows on the financial calculator.

| N | I/Y | PV | PMT | FV |
|---|---|---|---|---|
| 12 | 24 | -16,666.67 | 1,575.99 | 0 |

The difference paid to the note holder and the investor is $1421.76 per month. You can improve the yield if the owner of the mortgage you purchase will give you a discount, say anywhere between 10% to 15%. If you could negotiate a discount of 15% with the mortgage owner for the payment of one year's principal, it would appear as follows on the financial calculator.

| N | I/Y | PV | PMT | FV |
|---|-----|-----|-----|-----|
| 12 | 24 | -14,166.67 | 1,339.59 | 0 |

Your profit would be $1658.16 per month or $19,897.92 per year. Another possibility is to sell the 12 payments to the payer of the mortgage for a discount rather than to an investor.

If you paid the $1,658.16 per month against your $500,000 home mortgage you could either reduce your mortgage payments to $1,339.59 per month, or by applying all of the $1,658.16 to your mortgage payment, you would pay off your $500,000 home mortgage in 154.37 months. This would be a savings of $616,427.33 on your mortgage.

This example is predicated upon your ability to purchase 12 months of principal payments of a mortgage each year. You, of course, do not have to purchase principal payments on the same mortgages every year. Maybe, you can find a better mortgage to purchase each year.

What will you have accomplished with this technique? You are using the debt of another to pay off your own debt. A modification of this technique is to determine how soon you want to pay off your real estate. Then you purchase enough monthly cash flow to accomplish this goal. For example, if you wanted to pay off your house in one year rather than 30 years, you would need to purchase enough cash flow to produce the required monthly payments for 12 months.

For example, if you wanted to pay off your $300,000 mortgage in 12 months and your interest rate was 6%, you would need $25,819.93 per month. It would appear as follows on the financial calculator.

| House to be paid off in 12 months | | | | |
|---|---|---|---|---|
| N | I/Y | PV | PMT | FV |
| 12 | 6 | -300,000 | 25,819.93 | 0-Mortgage to be paid |
| Cash Flow Purchased | | | | |
| N | I/Y | PV | PMT | FV |
| 12 | 172.94 | -266,672 | 47,966.25 | 0-12 months of principal |
| Cash Flow Sold to Investors! | | | | |
| N | I/Y | PV | PMT | FV |
| 12 | 28.65 | -266,675.00 | 25,819.93 | 0-Investor's yield @28.65% |

The difference in the cash flow from the payments you purchased from the seller of the cash flow, and the amount you received from the investor of this cash flow which you sold him at a 28% yield is $25,819.93 per month. This is sufficient to pay your $300,000 mortgage in 12 months. The required payment would be $25,819.93 monthly. See the example above.

House loan: $300,000
Interest rate: 6.0%
New monthly payment: $25,819.93
Total amount saved over initial $300,000 principal at 6% interest over 30 years: $625,930.75.

# Notes:

# Technique #16

## Create a cash flow machine from land.

Have you ever turned down a deal to purchase land because there was no cash flow, or you could not afford to tie up the capital or assume the risk while the land appreciated? Try this technique to release the equity in land, and turn it into a cash flow machine.

You have located a nice 30-acre tract of mountain property for $2,500,000, which can easily be divided into 15 two-acre tracts, which should sell for $250,000 each. The seller is willing to owner finance, but requires a cash down payment of 25% or $625,000. You don't have either the down payment or the monthly payments. The solution is to create a note to the seller of the property, and offer to sell part of it to satisfy his cash requirements at closing. He agrees to finance $1,875,000 for 240 months at 8% interest with payments of $15,683.25 per month with a balloon payment of the balance in 10 years. This is the way it appears on a financial calculator.

| N | I/Y | PV | PMT | FV |
|---|---|---|---|---|
| 240 | 8 | -1,875,000 | 15,683.25 | 0 |

What about the down payment? Where does that come from? Buy half the payments (120 payments) at a 24% yield from the land seller and sell part of them, say 90 payments, to an investor for 12%. It looks like this on the financial calculator:

| N | I/Y | PV | PMT | FV |
|---|---|---|---|---|
| 120 | 24 | -711,319.96 | 15,683.25 | 0-Payments purchased |

Sell 90 payments to an investor at a 12% yield.

| N | I/Y | PV | PMT | FV |
|---|---|---|---|---|
| 90 | 12 | -927,834.97 | 15,683.25 | 0-Payments sold |

From the proceeds of the 90 payments sold to an investor, pay the down payment of $625,000. This leaves a remaining balance of $216,515.01, which can be used to pay the next 14 payments of the note.

During this period of time, subdivide the land into 15 tracts, sell the tracts for $250,000 each with 10% down, and finance $225,000 at 8% interest for 240 months. Use these notes as security for the payments to the original seller of the property, and sell off payments when needed to make any additional payments. For example:

| N | I/Y | PV | PMT | FV |
|---|---|---|---|---|
| 240 | 8 | -225,000 | 1,881.99 | 0-Original note |

| N | I/Y | PV | PMT | FV |
|---|---|---|---|---|
| 120 | 24 | -85,358.39 | 1,881.99 | 0-Buy part of note from seller |

| N | I/Y | PV | PMT | FV |
|---|---|---|---|---|
| 90 | 12 | -111,340.20 | 1,881.99 | 0-Resell part to investor |

The difference of $25,981.81 per note is the profit you make when you buy 120 payments from the land seller holding the note as security for your debt, and reselling 90 of those payments to another investor or institutional investor at the lesser 12% yield. If you have 15 notes, multiply this profit by 15 ($25,981.81 x 15 = $389,727.10). This will give you enough money to make almost 25 payments on your loan to the land seller. This will give you over two years of time to sell the lots at a profit.

# Technique #17

## How to buy a business with no money down and receive money at closing.

Everyone's dream is to be in business for himself. The challenge is the lack of capital to buy or start the business. Using the following technique, you can purchase a business utilizing discounted debt, and even get paid for doing it.

You have located a nice retail business for sale for $230,000 with a good cash flow. The owner is willing to finance if a buyer will put 30% or $69,000 down. She wants 10% interest on the balance of the purchase price and will finance for 15 years. The business will appraise for $450,000. You make the following offer: You offer to pay the seller the sum of $180,000 as a down payment at closing if the seller will take back a second mortgage for $50,000 at 10% interest for 180 months (15 years) with monthly payments of $537.30. The seller immediately accepts your offer. The problem is you don't have $180,000 or 80 cents. If you don't have it, somebody else does.

The solution is to create a mortgage and note, which can be discounted to an investor, which will yield the funds needed to close. If you created a note and mortgage for $230,000 (the asking price) at 10% interest, 180 months (15 years), with payments of $2,471.59 and sold the note simultaneously at closing to an institutional investor at a discount, you would create the funds necessary to close.

You found an institutional investor who was willing to purchase the note at a yield of 11.5%. Here is how it appears on the financial calculator.

| N | I/Y | PV | PMT | FV |
|---|---|---|---|---|
| 180 | 10 | -230,000 | 2,471.59 | 0-Original note |

| N | I/Y | PV | PMT | FV |
|---|---|---|---|---|
| 180 | 11.5 | -211,574.50 | 2,471.59 | 0-Note discounted to investor's required yield |

You arrive at closing. The note and mortgage and other closing papers are signed. The note from the buyer to the seller in the amount of $230,000 is then simultaneously assigned by an assignment document to the institutional investor. You sign the second mortgage in the amount of $50,000 to the seller as agreed. The $211,574.50 is wired into the closing agent's escrow account by the institutional investor. The seller is paid $180,000 as agreed.

Wait a minute. There is $31,574.50 left over. Where does that go? You guessed it. It goes into your bank account income tax free. Looks like the seller got her full asking price and $111,000 more than she originally was asking for in cash. In addition, you just purchased a business with no money down and got paid $31,574.50 for buying it through the technique of selling discounted debt.

# Buy a Business

- PURCHASE PRICE:

- $230,000.00

- $180,000.00 CASH DOWN

- $230,000.00 – 1ST MORTGAGE

- 10% INTEREST

- 180 MONTHS

- SOLD TO INSTITUTIONAL INVESTOR AT 11.5% YIELD

- PROCEEDS FROM SALE OF NOTE = $211,574.50

- OUT OF $211,574.00 PROCEEDS –

- PAY: $180,000 CASH TO CLOSE

- PLUS: $31,574.00 TO YOU

# Summary

- BOUGHT BUSINESS NOTHING DOWN

- POSITIVE CASH FLOW

- SELLER RECEIVES FULL ASKING PRICE

- $31,574.00 CASH IN POCKET AT CLOSING

# Notes:

# Technique #18

## Earn a million per year from somebody else's income stream.

This technique is not difficult to execute. However, it does require the ability to acquire a very large income stream such as a number of large commercial lease payments, structured settlements with large annual or monthly payments, government contracts payable monthly, or any other large monthly income stream. If you don't need a million dollars a year, you can always scale down the following numbers to fit your particular needs.

## Step One.

In order to create an annual income of $1 million per year, you will need to purchase a monthly income stream of $520,834 for 12 months at a 20% discount. That is, you will need to purchase 12 payments x $520,834 = $6,250,000 (per year) x .80% (20% discount) = $5,000,000. It appears as follows on the financial calculator.

| N | I/Y | PV | PMT | FV |
|---|---|---|---|---|
| 12 | 43.34 | -5,000,000 | 520,834 | 0 |

Your offer should be structured so that you will be able to buy 3 months of payments at a time for 4 times a year. In other words, you want to purchase $1,250,000 of the cash flow stream every 3 months. The monthly payments on this stream of income should be $520,834 per month. It appears as follows on the financial calculator.

| N | I/Y | PV | PMT | FV |
|---|---|---|---|---|
| 3 | 144.53 | -1,250,000 | 520,834 | 0 |

# Step Two.

Offer an investor a 25% return on his 3 months investment of $1,250,000 with the option to continue investing with you for a year (or more if it works out). It appears as follows on the financial calculator.

| N | I/Y | PV | PMT | FV |
|---|---|---|---|---|
| 3 | 25 | -1,250,000 | 434,147.09 | 0 |

The difference you receive from the cash flow\ stream of $520,834 per month and the $434,147.09 you pay to the investor each month for the use of his money at 25% is $86,686.91 per month or $1,040,242.92 per year. Well, I promised $1 million per year. You can give back the extra $40,242.92 if you like. If you can get by on a hundred thousand a year, just divide the numbers by 10. **Think Big!**

# Technique # 19

## Avoid foreclosures- buy high and sell low.

There are hundreds of courses that teach you how to buy properties near foreclosure, pre-foreclosure, short sales, and the like. People face unfortunate circumstances in life. People lose their jobs, are involved in accidents, or suffer illnesses, and get divorces. There needs to be a course on how to save one's home from foreclosure other than filing bankruptcy or some government bailout. This is not an attempt to provide such a course. However, this author does offer one technique which might provide a temporary solution to the potential delinquent mortgage, or at least one that can buy some extra time to seek a more permanent solution other than those provided by the loan sharks, foreclosure predators, and politicians running for office, offering government give away programs at tax payers' expense. For lack of a better title, I call it the Buy High - Sell Low technique. It sounds just the opposite of what we are taught in our economics classes in school.

However, I am speaking of purchasing a stream of mortgage payments on which you are currently paying, at a discount, and then simultaneously selling it to an investor at a greater discount. Suppose you are paying on an owner financed $100,000 mortgage with a 10-year term, at 8% interest, and payments of $1,213.28 per month. You are consistently late, because you have been laid off from work, but have been recalled to work and are in financial straits.

Offer the mortgagee (person receiving the payments) to pay a year's worth of payments in advance for a 20% discount. Realizing your financial condition, he would probably accept your offer immediately. The problem is you don't have a year's worth of payments. It is the next month's payment you are worrying about. The following is a possible solution in order to gain some much-needed time, and maybe some financial relief.

Offer to pay your next 12 mortgage payments in advance in exchange for a 20% discount. It appears as follows on the financial calculator.

| N | I/Y | PV | PMT | FV |
|---|-----|-----|-----|-----|
| 12 | 43.34 | -11,647.49 | 1,213.28 | 0 |

You would pay 12 payments of $1,213.28 x .80 (20% discount) = $11,647.49.

The next step is to sell these payments simultaneously to an investor for a 25% yield, or the best deal you can negotiate. It appears as follows on the financial calculator.

| N | I/Y | PV | PMT | FV |
|---|-----|-----|-----|-----|
| 12 | 25 | -12,765.43 | 1,213.28 | 0 |

The difference you would pay to the investor and your regular mortgage payment is $1,117.94. You will receive a little relief. However, offer to pay 3 months in advance for a 20% reduction and see what happens.

| N | I/Y | PV | PMT | FV |
|---|-----|-----|-----|-----|
| 3 | 144.53 | -2,911.87 | 1,213.28 | 0 |

| N | I/Y | PV | PMT | FV |
|---|-----|-----|-----|-----|
| 3 | 25 | -3,493.29 | 1,213.28 | 0-Pay towards investor's mortgage payments |

Buying and selling the income stream every three months would get the mortgage payments paid for one year, and would generate $581.41 in additional income every three months, which could go towards the mortgage payments.

# FOR THE INVESTOR

# Using paper to buy real estate

One of the most exciting and profitable aspects of discounted notes and mortgage investing is the different creative techniques one can utilize in buying real estate. The value of paper varies from person to person and changes with the economy. There is no secondary market where you can sell privately-held notes and mortgages like Fannie Mae, Ginny Mae, and Freddie Mac. Therefore, the value fluctuates from individual to individual. To many people, the value of paper is the face value. As we notes investors all know, this is not true. A great many people will accept a $25,000 note at face value, even though you may have bought it for $13,757.15.

Whenever a seller sells his real estate and agrees to take back a note and mortgage, he is, in effect agreeing to discount the value of his property, even though he might not realize it. Most people do not fully understand the concept of present value, and cannot see that they are discounting their property by taking paper in exchange for part of their equity.

Buying paper at a discount and trading it at face value to someone for their real estate creates tremendous profits. This can be done with both real and personal property. When this occurs, the discount is immediately realized in the property. Even though the seller may receive full price for his property, he just sold it for a discount.

**EXAMPLE:** The seller sells a parcel of real estate for $100,000. For purposes of simplicity, let's assume there was no down payment and the property is free and clear, and the seller is willing to take back a note for $100,000. If you were to buy a $100,000 note on a different property for $60,000 and trade it to our seller for full face value ($100,000), we would have effectively bought the seller's property for $60,000 (a 40% discount). Could you not then go to the mortgage company and get a loan on the property that you are buying at an 80% loan to value ratio? Then you pay the seller of the note the $60,000 agreed price at closing and put $20,000 in your pocket. Could this not all be done at a simultaneous closing?

Realistically, properties do not all sell for no money down, and they are not all free and clear, and you can't always find a note that exactly matches the seller's needs. However, if you understand the concept of substitution of collateral, the possibilities are endless of what you can do to acquire real estate at tremendous discounts, and terrific cash flows.

Here are five more ideas on utilizing discounted mortgages with substitution of collateral.

## 1.  NEGOTIATE A LOWER RATE THAN THE RATE ON THE NOTES

The notes being used as collateral (notes bought at a discount) could have a higher interest rate than the rate you are able to negotiate with the seller of the property.

## 2.  INCREASE THE YIELD ON THE NOTE BEING SUBSTITUTED PRIOR TO SUBSTITUTION

If the note you are going to use to substitute as collateral can be restructured to increase the yield, then, you can replace the note with another one that is comparable to the one you just improved.

## 3.  EARLY PAYOFF AND SUBSTITUTE

For example, if the note you have used as collateral has a face value of $10,000, which you bought for $6,000, you would still owe $10,000. However, you could negotiate with the payer to pay it off at a discount. If the note is paid off for say $9,000, then take $6,000 and buy another $10,000 note to substitute for collateral. This leaves you with $3,000, which is your profit.

## 4.  FORECLOSE

If the note goes into default, and you are well secured, you could foreclose and acquire a substantial equity. Could you not then create a new note against the property you just acquired in foreclosure?

## 5. CASH FLOW FROM DIFFERENT RATES

If there is a difference in the interest rates between the notes being used as collateral and your note to the seller, depending on how the notes are structured, the seller's note could pay off early or you could have a positive cash flow coming to you each month.

If you are interested in learning more about the fascinating business of investing, brokering, buying and selling real estate notes, check out the web site at:

**http://how-to-pay-off-mortgage-early.com.**

I especially recommend the comprehensive course in notes investing – Mega Mortgages.

# Notes:

_____

_____

_____

_____

_____

_____

_____

# Notes:

# Don't short circuit your short sales.

Can you profit from buying really bad real estate paper? When I use the word, term paper, I am of course speaking of notes and mortgages in the real estate world. Is it possible to pay a premium price for bad paper and still profit? The answer is yes, if you know what you are doing.

Too many real estate investors are shooting at the wrong target. They see the potential profits in the future appreciated value of real estate. I only know of two ways to increase the value of real estate without inflation in the economy. First, property can be increased in value by forced appreciation, i.e. fix up, rehabbing, re-zoning, etc. Second, you can "fix up" the financing. Own the financing, and you get a higher yield by restructuring the financing to increase the cash flow.

I was "cured" of "landlorditis" years ago, and I have found that the benefits of owing the paper are greater than the tribulations, trials, and terror of tenants, toilets, and trouble.

There are many ways to profit from defaulted paper. Behind every defaulted loan, there is a story. Inside that house is a distressed owner. It's your job to find out how that homeowner got into trouble, and how you can help him solve his problems. If you are not willing to go there, then stay away from the defaulted paper business. Treat the person in distress with respect. They are probably in denial. They are human beings. Please put yourself in their shoes. Help relieve their pain. It is the loss of a job, a divorce, an illness, or the poor management of money that got them there.

There are several ways you can help the person in distress.

1. Help the homeowner get a new start. Sometimes, they really can't afford the house anymore. Offer to pay the first and last month's rent on a new apartment they can afford. Catch up the payments on their overdue credit card, or car payments. Help

them with their hospital bills. Find them a dignified way to win in exchange for them deeding the property to you.

2. Take a deed in lieu of foreclosure, and pay all the back payments and taxes, plus some cash, to save their credit.

3. Help get the homeowner refinanced. This is where you come into the picture in a different way.

A possible solution is a relatively new twist to the old sell/ lease-back option where people need a lump sum of cash and, for some reason or another, cannot acquire the funds from a traditional bank or mortgage company. Let's assume a homeowner who needs cash approaches you. Here is a typical situation: A free and clear property. The value is determined by an appraisal to be $105,000. The seller/lessee feels that $750 per month including taxes and insurance is all he can pay. The taxes are $1,865 per year or $155.42 per month, rounded to $160. The insurance is $950 per year or $79.17, rounded to $80 per month. $750 rent - $160 taxes - $80 insurance = $510 per month. The seller is 3 months behind on all of his bills and credit cards and is approaching 2 months behind on his automobile. The seller would like to have $45,000.

Remember on our financial calculator that PV is the purchase price of the property. FV is the option price at the end of the lease.

Let's play "What If" with our calculator.

| N | I/Y | PV | PMT | FV |
|---|---|---|---|---|
| 36-pmts. On option | ? | -45,000 - purchase price | 510-monthly payment | 42,000 -option price |

| N | I/Y | PV | PMT | FV |
|---|---|---|---|---|
| 36 | 11.74 | -45,000 | 510 | 42,000 -option price |

Not bad, but nowhere near our goal of an 18% return.  Let's change the rate of return and solve for the purchase price.

| N | I/Y | PV | PMT | FV |
|---|---|---|---|---|
| 36 | 18 | 38,680  (purchase price) | 510 | 42,000  (option price) |

This is not working.  The seller/lessee is adamant that he can't pay more than $510 per month.

Let's reduce the amount of the purchase price and lengthen the term of the deal to 48 months.

| N | I/Y | PV | PMT | FV |
|---|---|---|---|---|
| 48 | 17.49 | -31,000 | 510 | 27,000 |

Pretty close.  Actually to get exactly an 18% yield, the rent would have to be $522.50.  We would round it to $520.  You could also increase the option price by allowing less than $1,000 per year credit against the option price from the lease payments, and keep the $510 per month lease payment.

How do you make money as an investor?  If the seller/lessee agrees to the above scenario, and you have an investor who will lend you money for a 10.5% return or some other acceptable return, you should proceed.  You decide that you want to make $2000 on the back end of the deal, and $60 per month during the next 48 months.  Let's see what the investor will pay for the income stream you have created.

| N Length of option | I/Y | PV | PMT | FV |
|---|---|---|---|---|
| Seller-48 | 18% | -31,000 | 510 | 27,900 |
| Investor-48 | 10.52% | -34,600 | 450 | 25,900 |
| You-48 | Infinite | -3,600 | 60 | 2,000 |

You can make a total of $8,480 over the term of the deal with none of your own money invested. The nice thing is the $3,600 is a non-taxable event because it is borrowed money. The $60 per month is partially offset by the interest on the loan from the investor, and it's possible that the $27,000 resale price might be a loss since your original basis was $31,000.

Of course, in the unlikely event the seller/lessee defaults on the lease and loses his option to repurchase his property, you can sell the property and make a nice profit.

This is a win-win-win. Win 1- The investor gets a safe management free real estate investment with a good return on his money and a chance for an even larger return in the event of default. Win 2- The seller/lessee finds the money he needs to solve his problems. He does not have to move, with the entire trauma it entails, and if he exercises the option or sells the property at a fair market value later, he does not suffer any loss. He repurchases his property for less than you bought it from him. Win 3- You, the investor, make money, and render a unique service in your community. Investing can be done with compassion for those in need. No need to short circuit any short sales by taking advantage of those in need.

# Invest in real estate, don't own it.

Short sales, subject-to, pre-foreclosures, bankruptcies, and rehabbing are real estate investing techniques with one commonality — all require the investor to make a payment to someone else. Acquiring equity in brick and mortar investments requires one to make payments to a lender if the property is financed. This further requires property management of tenants and maintenance, as well as the payment of taxes and insurance. The only cash flow comes from tenants or sales.

Why do investors use this investment model? A dog only does the tricks it is taught. The problem is if you always do what you have always done, you'll always get what you've always got.

Real estate investors are always taught that it is the normal and acceptable to make mortgage payments. I once heard a neighbor, a mortgage broker, say it was un-American not to have a mortgage payment. Many real estate agents and accountants push the "get-in-debt" theory by stressing the tax deductibility of the interest on mortgage debt. An old investor friend of mine who taught me the notes business, used to say, "What side of the mortgage do you want to be on?" Investors wish to own the wrong thing — the real estate, not the cash flow. I contend that most investors are on the "wrong side of the mortgage." They are always making mortgage payments instead of receiving payments.

What is a cash flow anyway? It's receiving payments, right? What's the difference between receiving payments from a mortgagor or a tenant? Have you ever wondered why the wealthiest people and institutions in the world are the lenders and not the borrowers? Have you ever wondered why an REO (real estate owned) by a bank is considered a liability rather than an asset on a bank's balance sheet?

Why does a bank get in trouble with the Federal Reserve and FDIC when its REO's reach a certain level? Why do banks have all the money? The reason is they lend money, albeit your money from your deposits, back to you at high interest rates. We are the only society that lends money to banks at low interest rates in the form of savings accounts and certificates of deposit at 1% and 2%. The bank, in turn, generously gives us a credit card, lends us back our own money at 18% to 30% interest, and charges us a late fee if we fail to pay our own money to it on time. No wonder banks give away toasters and suckers when you open an account. We are the toasted suckers.

Why invest in assets that we pay other people to own? Is it better to be lenders rather than borrowers? Is it better to invest in notes and mortgages rather than pay someone else to own them? Put simply, real estate is a tool to create cash flow. The object of the exercise is to convert real estate equity into cash flow, not the other way around.

When given the choice of receiving $100,000 in cash or $100,000 in equity in real estate, cash wins every time. Why is that? Money or cash is the universal medium of exchange. Cash is liquid, readily accepted, and recognized by law as the legal tender for the payment of all debts, both public and private.

Real estate represents a valuable asset, valuable because it provides a necessity — a place to live, work, and play. The value of real estate is measured in dollars, not dollars measured in real estate. Nobody says I want to exchange 100,000 bricks, 2,000 yards of concrete, and 1,400 square feet of roof for $250,000. It is always $250,000 for your building.

You don't go to an automobile dealership and say I will trade half of my duplex for your new Lexus or a grocery store and say I will give you one thirty-second of my rental unit for a week's groceries. Many investors are blinded by the trees and cannot find their way out of the forest. They lose sight of the ultimate goal and perform all manner of actions, some crazy or illegal, simply to acquire real estate without any thought of producing a cash flow or selling for a profit. Real estate, I say again, is simply a tool to create cash flow, not the other way around.

If you are convinced by my argument, let's examine the most efficient ways to create cash flow from real estate. Some of my investor friends choose rental properties; some choose to buy cheap properties, fix them up, and sell them; some choose to buy cheap properties, avoid the fix up, and sell at a higher price, also known as flipping. Regardless of the method you choose, foreclosures, flips, subject-to, short sales, or rehabbing, the result is the same. You own a piece of real estate. Everybody seems to overlook the most important element of every transaction — *cash flow*.

I am familiar with only three cash flows in the real estate investing arena. They are rent from tenants or lessees, cash from sales, and payments from notes secured by mortgages.

Have you ever considered that landlords are nothing more than collateral managers? They are managing real estate for the individual or entity holding the mortgage. Who generally receives the largest share of the income derived from the sale, rent, or lease of property? It is the mortgage company! Before the landlord, investor, repairman, insurance agent, or tax collector, the mortgage man is paid first.

Remember the old movie, "Silver Streak," when Richard Pryor told Gene Wilder, "Pay the man." It's the same thing in the real estate investing business. When it comes to the distribution of the proceeds at a closing, it's always, "pay the mortgage man." If you don't, in a very short period of time, you won't own the real estate anymore.

Invest in real estate — don't own it. Why would I recommend this? Because of its intrinsic value, real estate provides very valuable collateral for a cash flow investment. It is the collateral for the cash, and not cash for the collateral. If you are convinced by my argument, then why do I recommend notes and mortgages instead of property? The following are some of my favorite reasons.

- No tenants, toilets, troubles, or terrorists
- Always a positive cash flow
- Notes are liquid — easily sold, traded, or exchanged
- Never have to qualify for a loan
- Credit of the investor doesn't matter
- Investor doesn't need money to invest in notes
- Unlimited funding sources
- Passive income streams without management headaches
- Reduced risk
- Can fund with your IRA
- More creative

It never ceases to amaze me of the number of real estate investors who do not know how to calculate a cash flow, yield, rate of return on dollars invested, or how to operate a financial calculator. It is even more astonishing to see real estate investors buy real estate utilizing some method learned at an expensive seminar, which produces no cash flow at all. They are blindly taught to buy real estate for the sake of buying real estate without considering whether it produces a cash flow or not. Then, they wonder why their investment goes bad in a matter of months.

What makes real estate valuable as an investment? Is it the bricks or mortar, the intrinsic value, or the location? No, it is the cash flow. If real estate doesn't produce a cash flow, you must hold it until its value increases — making payments every month and tying up capital. If it is rental property, you must manage it, fix it, maintain it, and pay all the bills; whatever remains is the cash flow. Or you can buy cheap, run-down properties, or those from a distressed seller, fix them up at great expense, and sell them at a higher price, all the while making mortgage payments to someone else.

I maintain there is a better way to make money. Invest in the cash flow from the beginning; always insure you get paid first without the hassles of management, expensive loans, maintenance, vacancies, and so forth. What is the worst case? The buyer defaults on his payments. Your investment (the note and mortgage) is secured by real estate. You foreclose and sell it!

# Notes:

_____

_____

_____

_____

_____

_____

_____

_____

_____

# Notes:

# Let somebody else pay the mortgage on your home and pay you to live there.

Several years ago when I was into the landlord-tenant phase of investing, I heard an old experienced landlord say:" A good vacancy is better than a bad tenant." I never quite understood that statement until I had to dispossess a tenant, with all the attendant misery, aggravation, lost rent, and wasted time I spent in court. I could have spent that time as a lawyer on my paying client's cases.

Then I discovered the notes business. After I learned how to operate the financial calculator , and how mortgages really work, (stuff they don't teach you in law school), I discovered you could pay off your mortgage at an accelerated pace without making a mortgage payment from my own bank account, and make money each month without a tenant. SAY WHAT?

This is no misprint. It's called yield spread in the mortgage broker business or investing in discounted paper in the notes investing business. It works especially well if you have a property with a lot of equity and are going to refinance the property.

Most people refinance real estate to reduce the interest rate, reduce the payment, pull cash out to pay bills, or a combination of all three. All three are worthwhile objectives. Let me share a technique that I have taught for a number of years that was taught to me by an old notes investor years ago.

Let's use as an example, a house you own with an appraised value of $100,000. It has an old loan on it with a loan balance of $20,000, and payments of $587.01 per month. Don't get hung up on the numbers because we are going to pay this loan off, anyway.

We go to our favorite bank or savings and loan- the ones that give you a free toaster if you open a savings account that pays you a whopping 1.2% interest per annum. You have to deposit $10,000 and agree to leave it there for at least a year. You know the institutions I'm talking about. We obtain a plain vanilla 80% loan – to - value first mortgage of $80,000, interest rate of 6%, 30 years, with payments of $479.64 per month. Our closing attorney pays off the old loan balance of $20,000, and after we pay some closing costs, we have approximately $60,000 left over. We will exclude the closing costs for purposes of this example to make it simple.

We can now pay all our bills, go on a vacation, buy more expensive toys, invest in more real estate, or do something else. I recommend buying high yield notes and using the proceeds to pay off the new mortgage that you just signed up for at the United States Bank.

If you reinvested the $60,000 in a note or a combination of smaller notes to yield 24% for 120 months (10 years) you would generate $1,322.89 per month. Some skeptics will exclaim, "You can't do that." Experienced notes investors know it is being done every day, especially when utilizing partials (part of a mortgage).

Now here is the good part! Take all of the $1,322.89 you receive monthly from the notes you purchased and apply it to the new mortgage you just signed up for 30 years. What is the result? Your new 30-year mortgage will pay off in 72.19 months (6.02 years) instead of 360 months (30 years). Guess what? There are 48 months remaining on the $60,000 investment you made in the discounted notes. 48 months x $1,322.89= $63,498.72. You now have your home paid for in 6 years, and have an additional cash flow of $63,498.

You now have no mortgage payment after 6 years, a paid - for house that you can now live in, sell, or create a note against; and best of all you have no tenants to destroy your property or to dispossess. I wonder if that bank you borrowed the money from will give you another toaster if you put the $63,498 in your savings account.

# Rehab your notes for profits.

I was sitting in a meeting the other day across from a friend who is an expert in all phases of rehabbing houses. I was kidding him about being a "Commode Commander," a phrase I coined for rehabbers, from his recent article in a real estate publication called "Romancing the Commode." I then realized that we notes investors do the same thing, only that we do it with notes instead of houses.

One of the most exciting and creative things that a note investor can do is "rehab" or "re-cast" a note. It's very similar to buying a house and "fixing it up." When you rehab a house, you hope to increase the rents and increase the property's present value. Of course, you have to evict tenants, paint the property, add fixtures, replace plumbing, rewire, or do whatever is necessary to improve the property. You can do the same thing with a note without ever lifting a paintbrush or a hammer.

You can either sell the note, or keep it, and receive the additional income, which is a benefit of improving your note.

# Restructuring the note

When you buy a note at a discount, you can increase your yield on the cash flow. Several ways immediately come to mind. The possibilities are endless. First, you can increase the yield by increasing the amount of the payment you receive from the payer.

You can even offer to reduce the interest rate on the note to the payer. Here is how it works. For example, suppose you just purchased a note with 84 payments remaining, 10% interest, a present value of $50,000, and monthly payments of $830.06. You were able to purchase the note at a discount for $35,433.33, providing you a yield of 22%. It looks like this on the calculator.

| N | I/Y | PV | PMT | FV |
|---|-----|-----|------|-----|
| 84 | 22 | -35,433.33 | 830.06 | 0 |

Can you do any better than a 22% yield? Yes. You talk with the payer. He says he can afford to pay more. You agree to reduce his interest rate in half to 5%, if he will double his payments to $1,660.12 per month.

This is a very large increase in his monthly payment. Why would the payer agree to increase his monthly payments to this extent?

The answer: First, he will pay off the property in 35 months instead of 84 months. Second, he will save $16,440.84 in interest over the life of the loan. Third, he gets his interest rate cut in half from 10% to 5%.

Why would you, the note investor, agree to cut the payer's interest rate in half? Because you will increase your yield and get your discount back more quickly. Your new note, which you paid $35,433.33 (PV) as an investment, looks like this on the calculator.

| N | I/Y | PV | PMT | FV |
|---|-----|-----|------|-----|
| You will receive this number of payments on the new restructured loan | New yield | Cash paid for original note | Payer agrees to new payment | |
| 34.82 (35) months | 36.55 | -$35,433.33 | $1,660.33 | 0 |

You have increased your yield from 22% to 36.55%. You are happy. The note payer is happy. What happens if you bought the same $50,000 note for $35,433 and the payer paid it off in full the next day when he refinanced the property? Your profit would be $14,567, and your yield would probably crash your calculator.

Could you not afford to pay the discount points for the payer if he got a new loan, and paid your loan off? If this is not a possibility for the payer, get him to increase his payments by $25 per month. A $25 increase per month will reduce the 84-month loan to only 74 months. A $50 increase will reduce the term of the loan to 69 months, and a $100 increase per month will reduce the term of the loan to 62 months. Show him how many thousands of dollars in interest he will save.

Wrap the loan. If he needs money, offer to wrap the loan. For example, offer to lend him an extra $10,000 on top of the $50,000, but increase the interest rate from 10% to 12% on the entire note. Your effective yield is almost 32% on the entire loan. If this is not acceptable, you could offer to give the payer a 10% to 20% discount on the note if he would pay it off early.

Finally, you could offer to discount the amount he owes for every $100 he pays toward the principal. Advise him that he only needs to make extra payments when he has the money, and that he can always return to the old payment schedule.

You are missing a great opportunity if you are not constantly trying to improve your cash flow. As the old saying goes; "more sooner is better". You are increasing your yield, the note's present value, and your safety, since the equity grows, and the payer is less likely to default.

One last caveat (big lawyer word that means, "look out"), when you change the terms of a note, you create a new note which could become a second note behind someone's previous note. You could lose your priority. Contact an attorney when changing the terms of a note or mortgage. The attorney will insure that your new note maintains its priority.

# Notes:

# Short selling using discounted paper

Have you taken all the pre-foreclosure and short sale courses? Are you tired of dealing with the unresponsive bankers, and fighting off the competition that attended the same seminar you did? Would you like to make the banker and homeowner an offer they can't refuse?

Avoid the foreclosure process entirely and provide a win- win solution to the homeowner and the banker, and an ongoing cash flow profit to you, the investor, without mortgage payments from you or rent from a tenant.

Does the following scenario sound familiar? You have located a property with a $100,000 first bank held mortgage that is 3 months in default that is going into foreclosure. The property values in the neighborhood are rapidly declining. The property is only worth $90,000. There is no equity, and the banker just wants to "clean up the mess." He has received numerous offers from short sale investors. They are all too unacceptable.

Here is a different solution. Offer the banker an offer he can't refuse. You have located an investor who is willing to co-sign with you at the bank for a $75,000 note on reasonable terms. Note this is $25,000 less than the $100,000 note, which is now in default. Why in the world would a banker do this?

From the $75,000 loan proceeds, you purchase another note and mortgage or a combination of notes and mortgages at a discount upon terms similar to the new note you just acquired at the bank.

Buy the paper and trade it to the bank as additional security for the new loan. If you purchased the paper at a 15% yield, it would look as follows on the financial calculator.

| N | I/Y | PV | PMT | FV |
|---|---|---|---|---|
| 240 | 8 | -100,000 | 836.44 | 0-Note to be purchased |

| N | I/Y | PV | PMT | FV |
|---|---|---|---|---|
| 240 | 15 | -63,521.16 | 836.44 | 0-Same note purchased at 15% yield |

If you purchased the note or combination of notes for $63,500, you would have $11,500 remaining from the $75,000 loan proceeds that you could split with your investor, income tax free. You could enter into an agreement with the investor for a division of the equity in the property.

Let's go one step further. Since the bank is now receiving $836.44 cash flow each month from the note you have purchased at a discount and given as additional security, the new note at the bank ($75,000) will be paid off in half the specified time. It appears as follows on the financial calculator.

| N | I/Y | PV | PMT | FV |
|---|---|---|---|---|
| 240 | 6 | -75,000 | 537.32 | 0-New loan obtained from bank. Normal payment |

| N | I/Y | PV | PMT | FV |
|---|---|---|---|---|
| 119.26 | 6 | -75,000 | 836.44 | 0-Payment made from proceeds of note purchased |

The new loan is paid off in 120 payments (half the time), but there are 120 payments left on the note you bought at a discount. So, you continue to collect $836.44 per month for an additional 120 months or $100,372.80. You now have a paid-for house which you bought for no money down, and have made no payments, and have an additional $100,000 in cash with no tenants, toilets, terrorists, or trouble.

Want to make it a sweeter deal? Buy a partial note on a larger mortgage and you could pay off the house in 5 years or less rather than 10 years, and have more cash flow. For example, if you located a $300,000 owner carry back mortgage for sale with a 20-year amortization, 8% interest, and payments of $2,509.32, you could make it work by buying one fourth of the mortgage or 60 payments for your $75,000 loan proceeds. It appears as follows on the financial calculator.

| N | I/Y | PV | PMT | FV |
|---|-----|-----|------|-----|
| 240 | 8 | -300,000 | 2,509.32 | 0-Original note |

| N | I/Y | PV | PMT | FV |
|---|-----|-----|------|-----|
| 60 | 31.78 | -75,000 | 2,509.32 | 0-Partial purchased from $75,000 loan proceeds |

Then apply the $2,509.32 cash flow each month to the $75,000 loan you obtained at the bank to buy the foreclosure. It would pay off the bank loan in 32.45 months- less than three years. Amazing, but true!

| N | I/Y | PV | PMT | FV |
|---|-----|-----|------|-----|
| 32.45 | 6 | -75,000 | 2,509.32 | 0 |

There are 27 payments remaining on the partial you purchased for an additional $67,751.64 for your pocket.

You haven't made a mortgage payment yet.  Forget foreclosures.  Solve the problems.
The cash will flow after you.

# Notes:

_____

_____

_____

_____

_____

_____

_____

_____

_____

_____

# Real Estate Dictionary

ABSTRACT: A summary.

ABSTRACT OF JUDGMENT: A summary of a money judgment obtained in court. When this summary, or abstract is recorded in the county recorder's office, the judgment becomes a lien on the debtor's property, both presently owned or after acquired.

ACCELERATION CLAUSE: Clause in a deed of trust or mortgage, which "accelerates" - that is, hastens the time when the indebtedness becomes due. For example, some deeds of trust and mortgages contain an acceleration clause stating that the note shall become due immediately upon the sale of the land or upon failure to pay interest or an installment of principal and interest.

ACCOMMODATION RECORDING: Recording of instruments with the county recorder by a title company merely as a convenience to a customer and without assumption of responsibility for correctness or validity.

ACCRUE INTEREST: Allow interest payments to build up for later payment.

ACKNOWLEDGMENT: A formal declaration before a duly authorized officer (such as a notary public) by a person who has executed an instrument that such execution is his own. An acknowledgment is necessary to entitle an instrument (with certain specific exceptions) to be recorded to impart constructive notice of its contents and to entitle the instrument to be used as evidence without further proof. The certificate of acknowledgment is attached to the instrument or incorporated therein.

ADDENDUM: Additional parts of a note, usually on separate pages. Used for clauses that are not part of the printed contract. Also may be added anytime after the note was created to modify the note by specifying new agreements reached between the parties.

ADJUSTABLE RATE MORTGAGE (ARM): Mortgage in which the interest rate changes as a specified index's interest rate changes. Most often the mortgage payment will change upon each adjustment, but in some ARMS the payment remains fixed and interest accrues.

AFFIDAVIT: A written declaration made under oath.

AGREEMENT OF SALE: See Contract for Deed.

AGREEMENT TO CONVEY: See Contract for Deed.

ALTA SURVEY: See Survey.

AMORTIZED LOAN: A loan to be repaid, interest and principal, by a series of regular payments that are equal or nearly equal, without any special balloon payment prior to maturity.

AMORTIZATION: Reduction of a principal balance via payments over time.

AMORTIZATION TERM: The amount of time required to amortize the loan. The amortization term is expressed as a number of months. For example, for a 15-year fixed-rate mortgage, the amortization term is 180 months.

ANNUAL PERCENTAGE RATE ("A.P .R."): The cost of credit on a yearly basis, expressed as a percentage. Includes up- front costs paid to obtain the loan, and is, therefore, usually a higher amount than the interest rate stipulated in the mortgage note. This does not include title insurance, appraisal, and credit report.

ANNUITY: A contract pledging a series of payments over time.

APPRAISAL: An opinion of market value as of a specific date. This is required by most lenders to obtain a loan and by note investors.

APPURTENANT: Belonging to, accessory to. That is something incident to a chief or principal thing, as a right of way to land.

"ARB" OR "ARB NUMBERS": See Arbitrary Map.

ARBITRARY MAP: An office "subdivision" or map made by a title company for its own convenience in locating property in an area in which all the descriptions are by metes and bounds. On this "subdivision," the "lots" are given "arbitrary" numbers. The deeds and other instruments affecting these "lots" are posted to what is ca1 1ed an "arbitrary" account. The word "arbitrary" is often shortened to "arb."

ASSIGNEE: One who receives an assignment or transfer of rights. An assignment of a contract transfers the right to buy property.

ASSIGNMENT: Written document by which property - other than real property - is assigned, that is, transferred, from one person to another. Common assignments include contracts, leases, mortgages, deeds of trust and rentals. The "assignor" is the person who makes the assignment and the "assignee" receives the property assigned.

ASSIGNOR: The one who assigns to another person.

ASSUMPTION ("ASSUME A LOAN"): The purchaser of a property pledges to take, or assume, the place of the seller's liability on the existing loan. SEE SUBJECT TO.

ATTACHMENT: The seizing by the sheriff or other authorized officer of property belonging to the defendant as security for any judgment the plaintiff may get in a court action.

BALLOON PAYMENT: A lump sum payment on a note. It can be all or part of the remaining principal, accrued interest, or a combination.

BANKRUPTCY: A special proceeding under federal laws by which the property of a debtor is seized by the court and divided among his creditors.

BASIS POINT: A basis point is one one-hundredth of a percent For example; a 150 basis point rise in interest rate is the same as a 1.5% rise.  A 10 basis point fee is the same as a 0.1 % fee.

BEACON SCORE: A method of credit scoring.  See Credit Score and FICO Score.

BENEFICIARY: See Deed of Trust..

BINDER: A title insurance binder is the written commitment of a title insurance company to insure title to the property subject to the conditions and exclusions shown on the binder.

BLANKET MORTGAGE: A mortgage covering at least two pieces of real estate as security for the same mortgage, thus it "blankets" the properties.  This sort of loan is more common for commercial property or "special case" loans.

CALL: To require a balloon payment.

CAPITALIZATION RATE (CAP RATE): Net operating income divided by market value of the property.

CASH FLOW: Net income.

CERTIFICATE OF SATISFACTION: A document signed by the Note holder and recorded in the land records evidencing release of a deed of trust, mortgage, or other lien on the property.

CERTIFICATE OF TITLE: A statement provided by an abstract company, title company, or attorney stating that the title of real estate is legally held by the current owner.  The certificate does not certify as to matters not of record and affords no protection unless the author was negligent.

CHATTEL: Personal property.

CLAUSES: Separate sections of a note.

CLEAR TITLE: A title that is free of liens or legal questions as to ownership of the property.

CLOSING: The meeting, at which all documents for a transaction are signed, dated and notarized. Also called settlement.

CLOSING COSTS: Any fees paid by the borrowers or sellers during the closing of the mortgage loan. This normally includes an origination fee, discount points, attorney's fees, title insurance, survey, and any items, which must be prepaid, such as taxes and insurance escrow payments.

CLOUD ON TITLE: An evidence of encumbrances.

COLLATERAL: Assets pledged as security for a loan, such as property. The borrower risks losing the asset if the loan is not repaid according to the terms of the loan contract.

COMPARABLES ("COMPS"): The price at which properties comparable to the subject property have recently sold. "Listing comps" are asking prices of comparable properties that have not sold. When buying a loan, listing comps should not be used to determine value.

CONDEMNATION: The taking of private property by the government for public use - as for a street or a storm drain - upon making just compensation to the owner. (This right or power of government to take property for a necessary public use is called "eminent domain").

CONSTRUCTIVE NOTICE: Notice imparted by the public records, such as a newspaper notice, which legally notifies the parties involved. However, may not actually notify them.

CONTINGENCY (CONTINGENCY CLAUSE): A section of a note specifying that the note depends upon the satisfaction of the requirements stated in the clause.

CONTRACT FOR DEED: A written contract entered into between the seller (vendor) and buyer (vendee) for the sale of real property on an installment or deferred payment plan. The seller retains the deed and actual title (the buyer receives equitable title) and coveys the deed and actual title when the terms of the contract are fulfilled. It is also known as: Agreement to Convey; Land Contract; or Agreement of Sale.

CORPORATION: An entity authorized by law and endowed with certain rights, privileges, and duties of an individual.

CONVENTIONAL LOAN: A loan not guaranteed by a government agency. More commonly, a loan not involving the Veterans Administration, Federal Housing Authority, Farmers Home Administration, a state loan guarantee program, etc.

COVENANTS, CONDITIONS AND RESTRICTIONS: Commonly called "C.C. & R's," the term usually refers to a written recorded declaration or deed, which sets forth certain covenants, conditions, or restrictions established by a sub divider to create uniformity in a tract.

CREDIT HISTORY: A record of an individual's open and fully repaid debts. A credit history helps a lender to determine whether a potential borrower has a history of repaying debts in a timely manner.

CREDIT REPORT: A report of an individual's credit history prepared by a credit bureau and used by a lender in determining a loan applicant's creditworthiness.

CREDIT SCORE: A numerical indicator of an individual's credit history.

DEBT COVERAGE RATIO: A property's net operating income divided by its annual principal and interest payments.

DEBT SERVICE: 1. The principal and interest payments on a loan. 2. The total amount of credit card, auto, mortgage, or other debt upon which a loan applicant must pay.

DEBT-TO-INCOME RATIO: The ratio, expressed as a percentage, which results when a borrower's monthly payment obligation on long-term debts is divided by his or her gross monthly income.

DECREE OF DISTRIBUTION: A court decree, which determines how the estate of a decedent shall be distributed.

DEED: Written document by which land interest is transferred from one person to another. The person who transfers the interest is called the "grantor." The one who acquires the interest is called the "grantee." Deeds may be of many kinds. For example, there are grant deeds, administrators' deeds, executors' deeds, etc., depending on the language of the deed, the legal capacity of the grantor and other circumstances.

DEED IN LIEU OF FORECLOSURE: Requiring the mortgagor to sign over the deed to the note collateral to the lender. The deed is kept in escrow and not recorded unless the mortgagor violates the conditions of the note. In this case, it is recorded and the lender takes possession of the property, circumventing the time consuming and expensive foreclosure process. This procedure should be used with care: the mortgagor may sue under the theory of denial of due process.

DEED OF TRUST (TRUST DEED): Written document by which the title to property is conveyed as security for the repayment of a loan. In this document, the property owner is called the "trustor." The party to whom the legal title is conveyed (and who may be called on to conduct a sale thereof if the loan is not paid) is the "trustee. " The lender is the "beneficiary." A deed of trust is accompanied by a note outlining the terms of the loan and signed by the borrower (beneficiary). A deed of trust is unlike a mortgage in that the legal title to the property is conveyed to the trustee as security, while under a mortgage legal title to the property remains with the mortgagor. When the loan is paid off; the trustee is asked by the beneficiary to issue a "reconveyance," usually called a "recon." This re-conveyance corresponds to the release that the holder of a mortgage executes when the mortgage is paid off.

DEFAULT: Failure to make mortgage payments on a timely basis or to comply with other requirements of a mortgage.

DEFICIENCY JUDGMENT: A court ruling permitting a lender to attach a borrower's property other than the property securing the lender's loan. May be issued when foreclosure fails to produce enough to satisfy the loan balance and the borrower has pledged personal liability on the loan.

DESCRIPTION: A reference to maps, plats, instruments, etc., recorded in the county recorder's office or the federal land office upon which, by careful interpretation, the property can be located or identified.

DISCOUNT (A MORTGAGE): Purchasing for an amount less than the current balance of the note, obtained by calculating the present value of the stream of payments at a specified yield. For example, a note with a principal balance of $ I 0,000 that is discounted 20 percent would sell for $8,000 (20% of $10,000). The term is shunned by knowledgeable investors because it does not take the face interest rate or the payment schedule of the note into account A $10,000 note with a 12% face interest rate amortized over 10 years discounted 20 percent yields 17.9 percent The same note with a face interest of 9 percent at the same discount yields 14.5 percent The same note at 12 percent face interest but paid interest-only with a 10-year balloon at the same discount yields 16 percent Thus, "discount" can mean many things! SEE YIELD.

DISCOUNT SCHEDULE (A NONSENSE TERM): A rule-of-thumb used to discount notes. The most common is a discount of 5 percent from the principal for each year of the note. Thus, a 3-year note would be offered at a 15 percent discount to see why it is a nonsense term, SEE DISCOUNT.

DOWN PAYMENT: The difference between the purchase price and that portion of the purchase price being financed. Most lenders require the down payment to be paid from the buyer's own funds. Gifts from related parties are sometimes acceptable, and must be disclosed to the lender.

DRIVE-BY APPRAISAL: Also called a "windshield appraisal." An appraisal, which is done without the appraiser entering the property.

DUE-0N-SALE CLAUSE: A clause in a mortgage agreement providing that, if the mortgagor (the borrower) sells, transfers, or, in some instances, encumbers the property, the mortgagee (the lender) has the right to demand the outstanding balance in full.

EASEMENT: A right or interest in the land of another which entitles the holder to some use, privilege, or benefit, such as to place pole lines, pipelines or roads thereon.

EFFECTIVE INTEREST RATE: The cost of credit on a yearly basis expressed as a percentage. Includes up-front costs paid to obtain the loan, and is, therefore, usually a higher amount than the interest rate stipulated in the mortgage note. Useful in comparing loan programs with different rates and points.

EMINENT DOMAIN: See Condemnation.

ENCROACHMENT: Construction onto the property of another. When a building, a wall, a fence, or other fixture encroaches upon (overlaps) the land of an adjoining owner.

ENCUMBRANCE: A right or claim upon the real property (land) which does not hinder its conveyance or sale (transfer). Encumbrances are divided into two classes, as follows:

a. Liens (mortgages, deeds of trust, mechanics liens, local taxes, assessments, judgments, attachments, etc.).

b. Encumbrances other than liens, which are limitations on the ownership of the land (such as conditions, restrictions, reservations, easements, etc.).

ENDORSEMENT: Addition to a title insurance policy, which expands the coverage of the policy, fulfilling specific requirements of the insured.

EQUITY: The mortgage balance(s) subtracted from the fair market value of the property.

EQUITY LOAN: See Hard Money Loan.

ESCHEAT: A forfeiture of title to the state.

ESCROW: Delivery of a deed in which a third party acts as the agent for seller and buyer, or for the borrower and the lender carrying out the instructions of both, disbursing of papers and funds.

ESCROW ACCOUNT: (1) A third party's bank account to which he is contractually responsible for the interests of both other parties. (2) An impound account maintained by a lender for the payment of property taxes and insurance on a property.

ESTOPPEL: A signed statement from a mortgagor (note payer) verifying the principal balance, the interest paid to date, the next payment due date, the interest rate and the payment schedule. The estoppels should verify that there are no claims, defenses, rights, or offsets against the note.

EXECUTION: An order directing a sheriff, constable, marshal, or court-appointed commissioner to enforce a money judgment against a debtor. This officer levies on the debtor's property and, the sheriff may sell the property to satisfy the judgment.

EXECUTOR or EXECUTRIX: A man or woman appointed in a will to carry out its provisions.

FACTOR: A purchaser of accounts receivable.

FACTORING: Purchasing accounts receivable.

FICO SCORE: A numerical indicator of an individual's credit history. The lower the number, the worse the payment history. FICO stands for Fair, Issac and Company, the firm that developed this method of scoring.

FIRST MORTGAGE: A mortgage, which is in first lien position, taking priority over all other liens (which are financial encumbrances).

FIRST RIGHT OF REFUSAL: A clause in a note requiring the note holder, if he wishes to sell the note, to secure the best-written offer he can and then give the note payer the right to buy the note for that offer. Only after the note payer declines to buy the note can the holder sell it to another party. This is a critically important clause. When you are buying a note, be sure this clause is part of it. With it, you stand to profit greatly if the collateral is sold before your note matures (thus giving you a windfall profit when your note pays off early). Without this clause, you risk losing a great opportunity for profit.

FORECLOSURE: The legal proceeding under which a lender takes possession of the security for a note in default under a deed of trust; foreclosure is by public auction after appropriate advertisement A mortgage may require the lender to obtain Court approval prior to sale.

FORFEITURE OF TITLE: A common penalty for the violation of restrictions imposed by the seller upon the buyer in a deed. For example, a deed may be made upon the condition that if liquor is sold on the land, the title to the land will be forfeited (that is, lost) by the buyer (or some later owner) and will revert to the seller. (Actual reversion does not take place until a court decree has been obtained in an action brought against the landowner.)

FSBO: For Sale By Owner.

"GOOD FAITH" OR "MORTGAGE SAVINGS" CLAUSE: A clause which provides that "a violation thereof shall not defeat or render invalid the lien of any mortgage or deed of trust made in good faith and for value."

GRACE PERIOD: A period of time during which a loan payment may be paid after its due date but not incur a late penalty.

GRANTEE: See Deed.

GRANTOR: See Deed.

GROSS INCOME: The income of the mortgagor before taxes or expenses are deducted.

GUARDIAN: A person who is court-appointed to manage the affairs of a minor or incompetent person (called a "ward").

HARD MONEY LOAN (EQUITY LOAN): A loan in which the property equity serves as the sole qualifying factor. A hard money lender is generally unconcerned with such matters as the creditworthiness or income of the borrower.

HAZARD INSURANCE: A contract between purchaser and an insurer, to compensate the insured for loss of property due to hazards (fire, hail damage, etc.), for a premium.

HOMESTEAD: Under homestead laws enacted by a number of states, when a "declaration of homestead" is filed in the recorder's office the property described in this document becomes what is known as a homestead - the dwelling (house and adjacent land) of the head of a family. Thereafter, such property receives certain protections under the law from forced sale to satisfy creditor's claims.

HUD-I OR HUD SETTLEMENT STATEMENT: A form utilized at loan closing to itemize the costs associated with purchasing the home. Used universally by mandate of HUD, the Department of Housing and Urban Development.

HYPOTHECATE: To pledge something as security without delivery of the security to the lender. This is often used erroneously to mean borrowing money using a mortgage as the collateral. True hypothecation does not require the transfer of title to the security. When borrowing against a mortgage, be aware that lenders normally assess the financial strength of the borrower, rather than the note or income from the note itself, as the primary basis for their lending decisions.

INCOME STREAM: The payments on a note.  SEE CASH FLOW.

IMPROVEMENTS: Any part of a property that is not raw land.

INDEMNITY AGREEMENT: Agreement signed by an owner or builder/contractor to induce the title company to take an extended risk for a third party's benefit, usually the lender. Indemnity means "exemption from loss or damage."

INFERIOR LIEN: See Junior Lien.

INSTITUTIONAL INVESTOR: A company that purchases over $100 million in notes per year for its own account

INTEREST: A charge for borrowed money.  Also termed rent on borrowed money.

INTEREST -ONLY: Loan payments consisting entirely of interest, no principal.

INTERNAL RATE OF RETURN ("IRR"): That rate of return at which the present value of future cash flows is exactly equal to the initial capital investment.  Since income-producing investments (such as real estate) and certain note investments have future income streams of varying amounts and times, plus a lump sum upon distribution of the property, there are time disparities between the varying returns of and on the initial investment.  Since money has time value, the IRR can also be interpreted as "the rate each dollar invested earns during a given period."

INTESTATE: Without leaving a will or leaving, an invalid will so that the property of the estate passes by the laws of succession rather than by direction of the deceased.

INVESTMENT - TO-VALUE RATIO ("ITV"): The total amount invested plus the balances of any superior loans divided by the property value. For example, the ITV of a second mortgage purchased for $40,000 when there is a first mortgage with a $10,000 balance and a property value of $100,000 is $50"10$ (40+10=50/100=.50).

JOINER: Acting jointly with one or more persons.

JOINT TENANCY PROPERTY: See Ownership.

JUDGMENT: The decision of a court of law as to the rights of the parties in an action or proceeding. All judgments do not award money nor do they become liens upon real property when recorded.

JUDGMENT LIEN: A judgment is a lien against all real property owned by the judgment debtor in the county where the judgment is docketed (recorded).

JUNIOR LIEN: A loan in an inferior position to another loan on the same property, thus it will not be paid until the other loan, called the superior lien, is satisfied. See Superior Lien.

JURAT: A certificate evidencing that an affidavit was properly made before an authorized officer. It is also commonly and incorrectly used in trade language to mean an acknowledgement made on a separate form and attached to the instrument bearing the signature or signatures acknowledged.

JURISDICTION: The extent or legal right or authority to hear and determine a cause or causes. LAND CONTRACT: See Contract for Deed.

LEASE: Written document by which an owner of real property (lessor) gives the right of possession to another (lessee) for a specified period of time and for a stipulated rent.

"LEGAL": In property title insurance, a term meaning an insurable description.

LIABILITY (TITLE INSURANCE): The greatest amount of money an insurer will pay the persons insured under its policy, guarantee, or report in case of loss by reason of failure of title caused by defects against which they were protected there under.

LIEN: The right to take and hold or sell the property of a debtor as a security or payment for a debt The security interest created by a mortgage or other debt instrument against a property.

LIS PENDENS: Suit pending; notice of action.

LOAN COMMITMENT: A binding contract with a lender to issue a loan. A loan commitment usually specifies the interest rate (or it may "float," that is, may be locked in by the borrower at a future date) and an expiration date for the commitment.

LOAN CONSTANT: The annual principal and interest loan payment divided by the loan balance.

LOAN ORIGINATION: Making a loan. Purchasing an existing mortgage is not loan origination.

LOAN SERVICING: See Servicing.

LOAN-TO-VALUE RATIO (LTV): The total balance of all loans divided by the value of the property.

MECHANICS' LIEN: A lien upon a specific parcel of land to secure the compensation of those who, according to contract, have done work on or have been directly instrumental in its improvement.

MESNE: Intermediate; intervening.

METES AND BOUNDS (measurements and boundaries): When it becomes necessary to describe a parcel of land in an un-subdivided area or one that is a part of a larger lot, the parcel is described usually by metes and bounds, that is, by specific reference to the location, direction, and extent of its boundary lines. The starting point for such a description should be one that has been established by a recorded deed or official map.

MORTGAGE: A legal form of property lien. A written document by which land is put up as security for the repayment of a loan. This is determined by state law. In this document, the landowner is called the "mortgagor." The lender is the "mortgagee." A mortgage is accompanied by a note outlining the terms of the loan and signed by the mortgagee (borrower). A mortgage is unlike a deed of trust in that the legal title to the land remains with the mortgagor, while under a deed of trust the legal title is conveyed to the trustee as security. Its impact on note investors is principally in the foreclosure process, which is judicial under a mortgage and consequently more cumbersome and time-consuming than a deed of trust. Note that "mortgages" is often used generically to refer to mortgages, trust deeds, security deeds and land contracts. SEE DEED OF TRUST. SEE CONTRACT FOR DEED.

MORTGAGE BROKER: One who facilitates the origination of mortgages. A mortgage broker may also be, but is not necessarily, a note broker.

MORTGAGEE: The lender. SEE MORTGAGE.

MORTGAGOR: The borrower. SEE MORTGAGE.

NET OPERATING INCOME: Income less expenses, not including debt service.

NEGATIVE AMORTIZATION: Occurs when monthly payments are not large enough to pay all the interest due on the loan. This unpaid interest is added to the unpaid balance of the loan. The danger of negative amortization is that the homebuyer ends up owing more than the original amount of the loan.

NON-RECOURSE LOAN: In the event of default, the lender has no action available except foreclosure; he may not hold the mortgagor personally liable.

NOTE: Any written promise to pay. A negotiable note starts "Pay to the order of' and is transferable by endorsement similar to a check. A mortgage, security deed, or trust deed consists of two parts: the security instrument, which is the actual mortgage or deed of trust document encumbering the property. A note without a mortgage or other lien instrument is an "unsecured" or "promissory" note.

NOTE BROKER: One who purchases notes and sells them to investors. A note broker may also be, but is not necessarily a mortgage broker.

NOTICE OF ACTION: When a court action begins to affect the title or right of possession of real property, a notice of that action to the public may be recorded in the recorder's office. Also called "lis pendens".

NOTICE OF COMPLETION: Within ten days after a building is completed, the owner should file a notice to that effect in the recorder's office. The contractor and those who furnished material or worked on the building then have a certain amount of time within which to file their claims for unpaid bills. If such notice is not filed, claimants have a longer time within which to file. Before purchasing a lien on a new building or purchasing the actual building, the buyer should make sure that the Notice of Completion is filed and the time for claims has passed.

NOTICE OF DEFAULT: Notice given by the beneficiary under a deed of trust to the trustee showing that the trustor is in default (behind on the payments) and requesting that the trustee sell the property under the terms of trust to satisfy the debt.

NOTICE OF NON-RESPONSIBILITY: A notice (provided for by statute) filed by the owner of real property stating that he will not be responsible for any liability arising out of work being done on said real property by (or for) one holding an interest acquired from him (as where a lessee begins to erect a building or an oil derrick).

OMNIBUS CLAUSE: Clause in a decree of distribution by which "any other property not now known or discovered which may belong to said estate or in which said estate may have any interest" passes to the distributees named without specific description.

OPERATING EXPENSES: Property expenses other than those for financing and acquisition.

OPERATING EXPENSE RATIO: Annual operating expenses divided by the property annual income.

OPTION: A right given for a consideration to keep an offer to purchase or lease open for specific time.

ORDER CONFIRMING SALE: An order of the court confirming terms of the sale of an estate's assets.

OWNERSHIP: The right of one or more persons to possession of property to the exclusion of others. The incidents of property ownership are the rights to its possession, use, and enjoyment.

PAPER: Generic term for notes.

PARTNERSHIP: An association of two or more persons who have contracted to join in business and share the profits.

PARTY WALL: A wall erected on a property boundary for the common benefit and use of the two property owners on either side.

PATENT: A conveyance of title to government land by the government.

PAY-OFF AMOUNT: A total balance; amount of a full payment on existing loan or lien.

PERSONAL PROPERTY (movable): Any property that is not designated by law as real property (i.e. money, goods, evidences of debt, rights of action, furniture, automobiles, etc.).

P. I. Q.: A title term referring to property in question.

P I T I: Principal, interest, taxes and insurance, which comprise your monthly mortgage payment.

PLAT: A plan, map, or chart of a tract or town site dividing a parcel of land into lots.

"P. O. C." Term used on property settlement (closing) statements to refer to items paid outside of closing.

POINT: One percent of the loan amount, usually referring to the computation of a loan fee. For example, "9 percent and 3 points" means the loan interest rate is 9 percent and to obtain that loan the borrower will be charged a fee equivalent to 3 percent of the borrowed funds.

POWER OF ATTORNEY: A document by which one person (called the "principal") authorizes another person (called the "attorney-in fact") to act for him in designated transactions.

"PRE" OR "PRELIM": A written report issued by a title company preliminary to issuing title insurance, which shows the condition of title of the property in question.

PREPAYMENT PENALTY: A fee assessed for paying the balance of a loan before it is due to be paid.

PRINCIPAL: The amount borrowed and remaining unpaid on a note.

PRIORITY: Refers to the order of preference, rank, or position of the various liens and encumbrances affecting the title to a particular parcel of land. Usually the date and time of recording determines the relative priority, but in some states (i.e., California) the priority of mechanics' liens is determined by the time of commencement of labor.

PRIORITY INSPECTION: A title term referring to the type of inspection made in connection with insuring a new construction loan. In making the inspection of the property, the title company must be assured that the work of improvement had not yet begun when the lender's deed of trust was recorded.

PRIVATE INVESTOR: An individual that invests for his own account.

PROMISSORY NOTE: A written unsecured note promising to pay a specified amount of money on demand, transferable to a third party.

PURCHASE MONEY MORTGAGE: A mortgage, security deed, (or trust deed) created by seller financing of a property sale.

QUALIFYING RATIOS: Comparisons of a borrower's debts and gross monthly income.

QUIET TITLE: To free the title to a piece of land from the claims of other persons by means of a court action is called a "quiet title" action. The court decree obtained is a "quiet title" decree.

REAL PROPERTY (immovable): Land from the center of the earth and above the surface indefinitely; that which is affixed to land; that which is incidental or appurtenant to land. Examples: minerals, trees, buildings, appurtenant rights, etc.

"RECON" OR RE-CONVEYANCE: See Deed of Trust

RECORDING: The filing of a document with the county recorder for the purpose of having it copied into the public records. The recording of a document gives notice to the public of its contents.

RECOURSE: When a mortgage, trust deed or other note is sold "With Recourse," the seller is guaranteeing the payments and making himself personally liable for the performance of the mortgagor.

REDEMPTION PERIOD: The time legally allotted to a mortgagor to repurchase the property that the mortgagee foreclosed upon. Varies by state law from one year after foreclosure to nothing (no right of redemption). Mortgage investors usually avoid buying mortgages in states with long rights of redemption.

REFINANCE: To borrow money and thus to create a new loan against a property to satisfy an existing indebtedness.

REGULATION Z OR REG Z: See Truth-In-Lending Act.

RELEASE CLAUSE: Language in a loan document describing the terms under which the borrower may have part of the collateral released from the lien.

RESPA: Short for the Real Estate Settlement Procedures Act RESPA is a federal law that allows consumers to review information on known or estimated settlement costs once after application and once prior to or at a settlement; the law requires lenders to furnish the information after application only.

RIGHT OF RESCISSION: The legal right to void or cancel a mortgage in such a way as to treat the mortgage as if it never existed. Right of rescission is not applicable to mortgages made to purchase a home, but may be applicable to other mortgages, such as home equity loans.

RIGHT OF REDEMPTION: Allowing a mortgagor to repurchase a property that has been foreclosed upon. In some jurisdictions, this may be a one-year period.

RIGHT OF WAY: Right to cross a parcel of land.

RULE OF 78s: A loan amortization method that lumps the interest to be paid over the life of the loan into the early years of the loan, creating a loan balance for those years greater than the amount borrowed. Thus, an early payment of the balance due on a loan calculated under the Rule of 78s can easily result in the borrower having to pay back more than he borrowed.

SECOND LIEN: A mortgage, deed of trust or other lien junior to another in first position. See Junior Lien.

SECONDARY MARKET: A market for the purpose of purchase and sale of existing mortgages usually at discounted prices to provide greater liquidity to the mortgagee/lender.

SECURITY INTEREST: An interest that a lender takes in the borrower's property to assure repayment of a debt.

SEPARATE PROPERTY: See Ownership.

SERVICING: Collecting loan payments. Servicing may also include making property tax and hazard insurance payments when due, issuing late payment letters, collection and foreclosure processing.

SETTLEMENT: See Structured Settlement See Closing.

SUBJECT TO: A property sale in which the seller remains liable for the repayment of the existing loan.

SUBORDINATE: To make a lien inferior to another lien.

SUBSTITUTION OF COLLATERAL: To replace one property with another as the security for a loan.

SUPERIOR LIEN: A loan in a higher position relative to another loan on the same property. A first mortgage is superior to a second mortgage. It must be paid before the inferior, or junior, lien is paid. SEE JUNIOR LIEN.

STARTER: A copy of the last policy or report issued by a title insurer, which described the land upon which a new search is to be made.

STREET IMPROVEMENT BONDS: Interest-bearing bonds issued, usually by a city or county, to secure the payment of assessments levied against land to pay for street improvements. The property owner may pay off the particular assessment against his property, or he may allow the assessment to "go to bond."

SUBORDINATION AGREEMENT: An agreement by which one encumbrance (for example, a mortgage) is made subject to another encumbrance (perhaps a lease). To "subordinate" is to "make subject to.

SURFACE RIGHTS: Rights to enter upon and use the surface of a parcel of land, usually in connection with an oil and gas lease. Sometimes they are "implied" by the language of the lease (no explicit reservation or exception of the surface rights) and other times they are "explicitly" set forth.

SURVEY: The measurement, which delineates the boundaries of a parcel of land determined by a surveyor. An ALTA survey additionally delineates the exact location of all improvements, encroachments, easements and other matters affecting the title to the property in question.

TESTATE: A decedent who has left a written declaration of his or her last will.

TITLE: The written evidence that proves the right of ownership of a specific piece of property.

TITLE COMMITMENT: A binding contract with a title company to issue a specific title policy, showing only those exceptions contained in the commitment and any intervening matters after the date of the commitment and prior to the effective date of the policy. The commitment contains all information included in the preliminary title report, plus a list of the title company's requirements to insure the transaction. It also includes the standard exceptions to coverage that will appear in the policy.

TITLE INSURANCE: Protection for lenders or homeowners against financial loss resulting from legal defects in the title.

TITLE SEARCH: An investigation into the history of ownership of a property to check for liens, unpaid claims, restrictions, or problems, to prove that the seller can transfer fee and clear ownership.

TOTAL DEBT RATIO: Monthly debt and housing payments, divided by gross monthly income.

TRUST DEED: See Deed of Trust..

TRUSTEE: See Deed of Trust.

TRUSTOR: See Deed of Trust.

TRUTH-IN-LENDING ACT: A federal law requiring a disclosure of credit terms using a standard format. This is intended to facilitate comparisons between the lending terms of different financial institutions. Also known as Regulation Z or "Reg Z."

UNDERWRITING: The process of verifying data and approving a loan.

UNSECURED NOTE: A note not secured by a lien instrument .This is actually a misnomer, since in the absence of a specific lien, the note holder can sue for satisfaction of the debt and claim any or all of the debtor's property.

USURY: Charging an interest rate for a loan higher than the legal maximum. State laws determine usury.

VENDEE: See Contract for Deed.

VENDOR: See Contract for Deed.

VENUE: Neighborhood; often used to refer to the county or place in which an acknowledgment is made before a notary; also refers to the county in which a lawsuit may be filed or tried.

VESTING: The names, status, and manner in which title of ownership is held with a fixed or determinable interest in a particular parcel of real property; also that portion of a title report or policy setting forth the above.

WAIVE: To release or abandon - as to "waive" a right of appeal from a court decree.

WINDSHIELD APPRAISAL: See Drive-By Appraisal.

WRAP (WRAP AROUND; A.I.T.D. ["All Inclusive Trust Deed]): A combination of a senior and junior lien in which the lender collects one payment from the borrower, makes the payment on the senior lien and retains the balance as the payment on the junior lien.

YIELD: The return from an investment expressed as a percentage, it is the rate of interest earned on the money invested. To a knowledgeable investor, it is the key factor governing every note transaction.

# Illustrations

# Promissory Note

<u>$  (Amount)  </u>    <u>          (Place)              </u>    <u>    (Date)      </u>    pay to the
order of _____the principal
sum of _____dollars ($_____)
together with interest thereon from this date at the rate of _____ percent per annum until
maturity.  The said principal and interest being payable at _____
or at such other place as the holder hereof may designate in writing.  The said principal and
interest being payable as follows:

(Here include the specific terms of the note.)

This note may be prepaid in whole or in part at any time without penalty.

This note is secured by a mortgage of even date herewith and is to be construed and enforced according to the laws of the State of _____.  Upon the makers' failure to pay any sum required to be paid by the terms of this note or the securing mortgage, promptly when they severally become due, or upon the breach of any stipulation, agreement or covenant of this note or of the securing mortgage, the entire sum of principal and interest remaining unpaid balance shall, at the option of the holder hereof, become immediately due and payable.  Failure to exercise said option shall not constitute a waiver of the right to exercise the same at any subsequent time.

This note, including any installment payment of principal and/or interest, shall bear interest at the rate of _____% per annum from the respective maturity dates thereof until paid.

Each maker and endorser agrees, jointly and severally, to pay all cost of collection, including a reasonable attorney's fee, if this note, including any installment payment, is not paid promptly when due, and the same is given to any attorney for collection, whether suit be brought or not.

Each maker and endorser severally waives demand, protest, and notice of maturity, non-payment, or protest and notice of maturity, non-payment or protest and all other requirements necessary to hold each of them liable as makers and endorsers

_____(Seal)

_____(Seal)

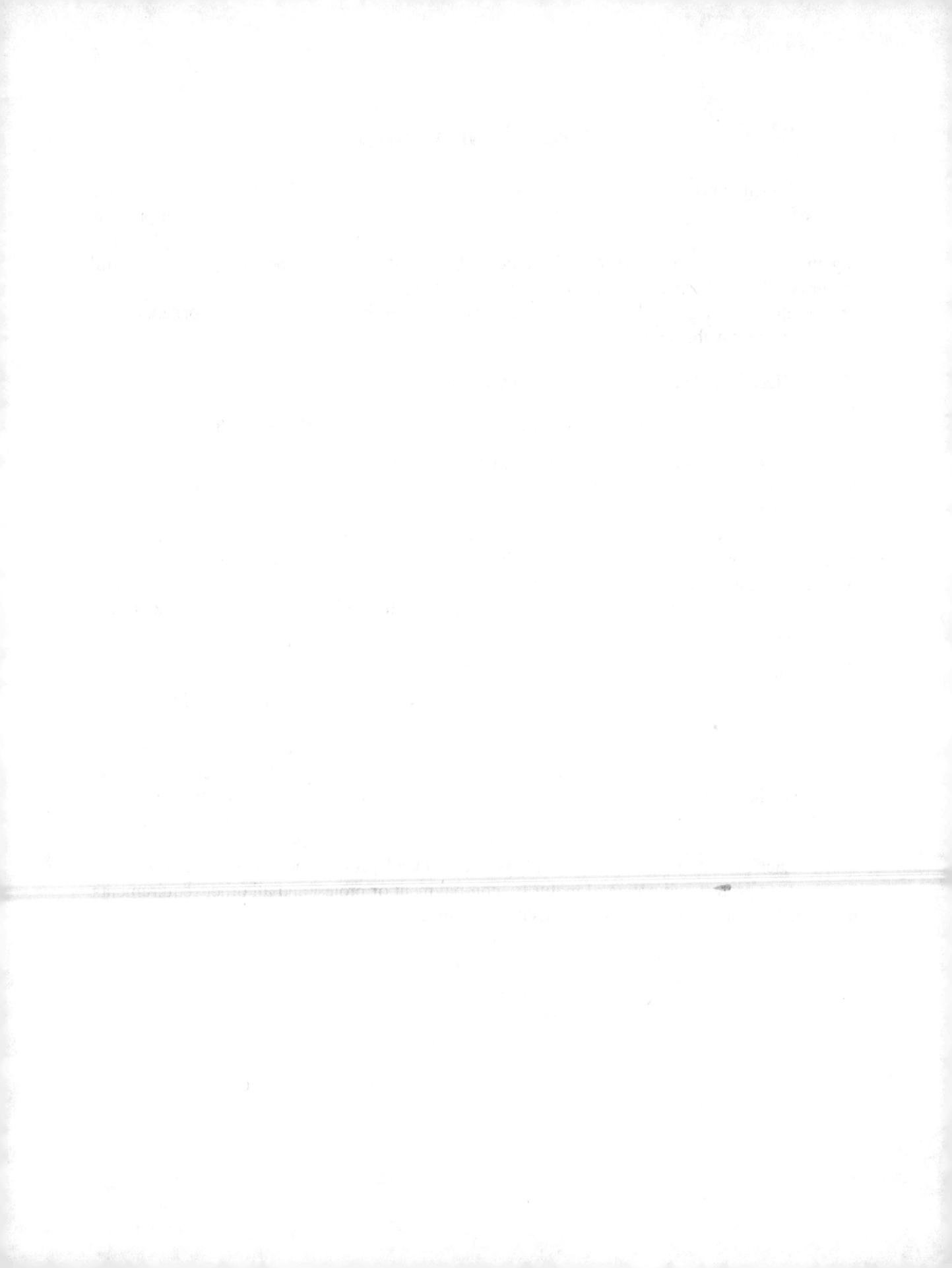

# Additional Payment Letter

United States Bank of America
1234 Bailout Drive
Mortgage City, USA

In Re: Loan Number _____

(Name(s) on Loan)

(Street Address of Property, City State, Zip)

Gentleman:

Please find enclosed two (2) checks for payment on the above loan.

One check is for my regular payment of $_____(regular mortgage payment). The second check in the amount of $_____ is payment of additional principal. This payment is to be applied to the next payment, and not to the last payment, or payment into my escrow account (if applicable) and sequential adjacent payments until all of the extra payment is used.

If you have any questions, please call me at (your telephone number).

Very truly yours,

_____

Mortgage Payer

# Mortgage

## Short Form

**THIS INDENTURE**, made this _____ day of _____, A.D. 20____,
**BETWEEN** _____ hereinafter called the Mortgagor, and
_____ hereinafter called the Mortgagee,

**WITNESSETH**, that the said Mortgagor, for and in consideration of the sum of One Dollar, to _____ in hand paid by the said Mortgagee, the receipt whereof is hereby acknowledged, granted, bargained and sold to the said Mortgagee, ____ _____ heirs and assigns forever, the following described land situate, lying, and being in the County of _____, State of _____, to wit: _(deed description)_ and the said Mortgagor does hereby fully warrant the title to said land, and will defend the same against the lawful claims of all persons whomsoever.

**PROVIDED ALWAYS**, that if said Mortgagor, _____ heirs, legal representatives or assigns shall pay unto the said Mortgagee, _____ legal representatives or assigns, certain promissory note dated the _____ day of_____, A.D. 20_____, for the sum of _____dollars, payable _____ with interest at _____ percent from _____ signed by _____ and shall perform, comply with and abide by each this mortgage, and shall pay all taxes which may accrue on said land and all costs and expenses said Mortgagee may be put to in collecting said promissory note by foreclosure of this mortgage or otherwise, including a reasonable attorney's fee, then this mortgage and the estate hereby created shall cease and be null and void.

**IN WITNESS WHEREOF**, the said Mortgagor hereunto set _____hand and seal _____ the day and year first above written.

Signed, sealed, and delivered in presence of us:

(_____)     _____ (SEAL)


(_____)     _____ (SEAL

# Credit Report Authorization

Date: _____

To: _____ (Any credit reporting agency)

To enable (Seller)_____ to make a final decision concerning the sale of their property to us on terms, we are providing our social security numbers and authorize you to issue the Sellers a Credit Report on us.


**Name of Buyer (#1)**: _____

Social Security Number: _____

**Current Home** Street Address:_____

City, State, Zip: _____

Home Phone:_____ Cell Phone:_____

Work Phone: _____

**Previous Home Address (within the last five years)**:

Street Address:_____

City, State, Zip: _____

**Current employer**: _____

Street Address: _____

City, State, Zip: _____ Phone: _____

**Date:** _____ **Signature**: _____


**Name of Buyer (#2)**: _____

Social Security Number: _____

**Current Home** Street Address:_____

City, State, Zip: _____

Home Phone:_____ Cell Phone:_____

Work Phone: _____

**Buyer (#2):**

**Previous Home Address (within the last five years):**

Street Address:_____

City, State, Zip: _____

**Current employer**: _____

Street Address: _____

City, State, Zip: _____ Phone: _____

**Date:** _____ **Signature**: _____

# INDEX

# BOOKS, COURSES

## and

## SEMINARS

## By

## E. Wright Davis

# Getting Started in Creative Real Estate Investing

### Book by E. Wright Davis

Learn 21 of the most creative real estate investing techniques ever known.

This is the only manual you will ever need when it comes to creative real estate investing and finance. Most of the techniques taught utilize owner financing and very little conventional bank financing.

**Some of the techniques you will learn from this book containing forms and examples of typical contract clauses:**

√   Cash to existing mortgage.

√   Paper out offer.

√   Seller refinance with a first mortgage crank.

√   Seller refinance with a second mortgage crank.

√   Created paper down payment.

√   Paper out offer subject to seller trading paper.

√   Blanket mortgage combined with a second mortgage crank.

√   Lease with option to purchase.

√   Reverse interest loan offer.

√   Paper used as substituted collateral

√   Contract clauses, forms and techniques to pay off your mortgage fast.

√   MANY more techniques.

**Cost:  $39 (plus shipping and handling)**

# *Mega Mortgages*

## 4-Day DVD Seminar conducted by E. Wright Davis

Mega Mortgages is a comprehensive course on the Cash-Flow Industry. This four-day DVD course will take the student from grammar school to graduate school in cash flow investing.

**In this course, you will learn:**

√ The basics of discounted notes and mortgages.

√ How the principles of the time value of money will make you wealthy.

√ How to find, buy, and sell notes for big profits.

√ How to buy real estate at a discount with no money down, a positive cash flow and put money in your pocket at closing.

√ How to pay off your house in 5 years without having to make a house payment.

√ How to receive 31+% yield on notes using none of your own money.

√ How to buy notes with no money down.

√ How to get free notes without foreclosures, short sales or hard money loans.

√ How to get a free $80,000 IRA.

√ How to buy a business with notes.

√ How to get a free house.

√ Eliminate the risks.

√ How to use the financial calculator.

√ Partial purchases.

√ Note possibilities.

√ Marketing.

√ The nuts, bolts and paperwork.

√ Nitch markets.

√ The law and the discount paper business.

**With this course you will receive:**

√ DVD copies of a live 4-day presentation by E. Wright Davis of *Mega Mortgages, Calculator Power!* and *How To Crack the Mortgage Code.*

√ *How to Crack The Mortgage Code…* A complete manual containing forms…………… a $69 value.

√ *Mega Mortgages…* A complete manual containing forms and a DVD live presentation… a $1,295 value.

√ *Getting Started in Creative Real Estate Investing…* this manual contains forms and a list of examples of typical contract clauses… a $39 value.

√ *Calculator Power!* A complete manual. A simple hands on guide to using a financial calculator– a $249 value.

If the above items were to be purchased separately, the cost would be $1,652.

**The cost for this 4-day seminar <u>including all of the items above</u>:**

**$695…. a savings of $957**

# *Calculator Power*
## By Jon Richards and David Roberts
## Course by E. Wright Davis
## (Included as a BONUS in the seminar package)

This is the most comprehensive real estate finance course ever.

This manual and the accompanying FREE DVD's will give you all the hands on step-by-step instruction on every aspect of the operation of the financial calculator you will ever need.

This is a full 8-hour course with comprehensive easy to understand instructions.

**With this course, you will learn how to:**

√ Structure offers to buy real estate.

√ Structure real estate financing utilizing the concepts of the time value of money.

√ A step-by-step approach to calculating payments on a loan.

√ Calculate the remaining balance due on a mortgage.

√ Calculate balloon payments.

√ Calculate time value of money concepts.

√ Calculate the present value of streams of real estate income.

√ Calculate discount real estate income to present value.

√ Make offers that will insure more closing utilizing these concepts.

**Cost:  $249 Plus shipping and handling.**

# To Place Your Book Order

## On the internet or by phone:

Information for ordering E. Wright Davis's books on the internet or by phone using a credit card or PayPal can be found at:

www.ewrightdavis.com

---

# Viewing Live Streaming Seminars & Webinars

# via the Internet

To view live streaming seminars and/or webinars via the internet, complete instructions to sign up with details regarding dates, times and registration fees can be found at:

www.ewrightdavis.com

---

# Attending E. Wright Davis's Live Seminars in person

To attend one of E. Wright Davis's live seminars in person, complete details regarding location, dates, times and registration fees can be found at:

www.ewrightdavis.com